W9-AAZ-033

Pocket
İSTANBUL

TOP SIGHTS • LOCAL LIFE • MADE EASY

Virginia Maxwell

In This Book

QuickStart Guide

Your keys to understanding the city – we help you decide what to do and how to do it

Need to Know
Tips for a smooth trip

Neighbourhoods
What's where

Explore İstanbul

The best things to see and do, neighbourhood by neighbourhood

Top Sights
Make the most of your visit

Local Life
The insider's city

The Best of İstanbul

The city's highlights in handy lists to help you plan

Best Walks
See the city on foot

İstanbul's Best...
The best experiences

Survival Guide

Tips and tricks for a seamless, hassle-free city experience

Getting Around
Travel like a local

Essential Information
Including where to stay

Our selection of the city's best places to eat, drink and experience:

⊙ **Sights**

⊗ **Eating**

⊜ **Drinking**

✪ **Entertainment**

⊙ **Shopping**

··

These symbols give you the vital information for each listing:

☎ Telephone Numbers		👪	Family-Friendly
⊙ Opening Hours		🐾	Pet-Friendly
P Parking		🚌	Bus
⊝ Nonsmoking		⛴	Ferry
@ Internet Access		M	Metro
🛜 Wi-Fi Access		S	Subway
🥗 Vegetarian Selection		🚊	Tram
📖 English-Language Menu		🚆	Train

··

Find each listing quickly on maps for each neighbourhood:

Bar Hemingway

16 ⊜ Map p233, B2

Legend has it that Hemi self, wielding a machine rate this timber-pan ered bar during showpiece is a en by Papa ar town. Dress s.com; Hôtel Rit ; ⊙6.30pm-2a

Lonely Planet's İstanbul

Lonely Planet Pocket Guides are designed to get you straight to the heart of the city.

Inside you'll find all the must-see sights, plus tips to make your visit to each one really memorable. We've split the city into easy-to-navigate neighbourhoods and provided clear maps so you'll find your way around with ease. Our expert authors have searched out the best of the city: walks, food, nightlife and shopping, to name a few. Because you want to explore, our 'Local Life' pages will take you to some of the most exciting areas to experience the real İstanbul.

And of course you'll find all the practical tips you need for a smooth trip: itineraries for short visits, how to get around, and how much to tip the guy who serves you a drink at the end of a long day's exploration.

It's your guarantee of a really great experience.

Our Promise

You can trust our travel information because Lonely Planet authors visit the places we write about, each and every edition. We never accept freebies for positive coverage, so you can rely on us to tell it like it is.

QuickStart Guide 7

Explore İstanbul 21

Worth a Trip:

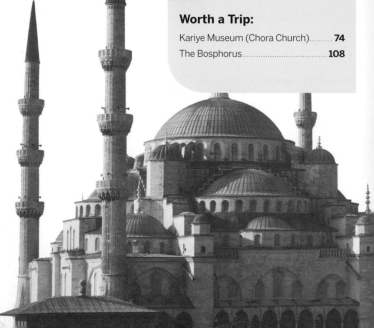

QuickStart Guide

Welcome to İstanbul

In İstanbul, extraordinary experiences are found around every corner. Here, dervishes whirl, *müezzins* call from minarets and people move between continents multiple times a day. Home to millennia-old monuments and cutting-edge art galleries (sometimes in the same block), it's a destination where eating, drinking and dancing are local priorities, and where everyone is welcome to join the party.

Food stalls near the New Mosque (p66)
MATT MUNRO/LONELY PLANET ©

⊙ İstanbul Top Sights

Aya Sofya (p24)

History resonates when you visit this majestic basilica. Built in the 6th century AD, its remarkable features include a massive dome and a stunning collection of Byzantine mosaic portraits.

Topkapı Palace (p42)

A series of mad, sad and downright bad sultans lived in this pavilion-style palace during the glory days of the Ottoman Empire. Reminders of their privileged lifestyles are everywhere to be seen.

The Bosphorus (p108)

A ferry trip down the mighty Bosphorus strait showcases a passing parade of mosques, palaces and mansions on both the Asian and European shores.

Grand Bazaar (p56)

Sometimes described as the world's oldest and most evocative shopping mall, this colourful and chaotic covered market is the heart of İstanbul's Old City and one of its most atmospheric destinations.

Kariye Museum (Chora Church; p74)

Great things can come in small packages. This diminutive Byzantine church is made extraordinary by virtue of its interior, which is crammed with exquisite mosaics and frescoes.

İstanbul Archaeology Museums (p46)

An eclectic and exhilarating collection of antiquities, classical sculpture, Ottoman tilework and Byzantine artefacts is showcased at this museum complex next to Topkapı Palace.

Süleymaniye Mosque (p60)

Truly deserving the tag 'living history', this imperial mosque atop the city's fourth hill is one of few that has retained, restored and creatively reused its original outbuildings.

İstiklal Caddesi (p78)

A promenade down this pedestrianised 19th-century boulevard is the quintessential İstanbul experience, offering a colourful snapshot of local life.

İstanbul Modern (p80)

İstanbul has one of the most exciting contemporary art scenes in the world, and this gallery housed in a converted shipping warehouse on the Bosphorus is its pre-eminent venue. (Below: *False Ceiling* by Richard Wentworth)

Dolmabahçe Palace (p100)

This palace on the Bosphorus shore – built as the Ottoman Empire's power waned but making no concessions to this fact – gives a fascinating glimpse into the artificial lives and ostentatious taste of the sultans.

Basilica Cistern (p30)

Both architectural tour de force and virtuosic engineering feat, this evocatively lit underground cistern is one of İstanbul's most mysterious and magnificent Byzantine monuments.

Blue Mosque (p28)

Beloved of tourists and locals alike, the most photogenic of İstanbul's imperial mosques is also one of the busiest places of worship in the city.

İstanbul Local Life

Insider tips to help you find the real city

İstanbul's 14 million residents enjoy an exhilarating lifestyle that is crammed with culture, against the backdrop of history and underpinned by family and faith. Head to their neighbourhoods, mosques, shops and cafes to see what makes life here so special.

Between the Bazaars (p62)

▶ Local shopping
▶ Historic buildings

The winding streets linking the historic Grand and Spice Bazaars are crammed with İstanbullus every day of the week except Sunday. Locals have purchased provisions, outfitted themselves and stocked up on household goods of every possible description here for centuries, and most show no sign of moving their custom to the soulless shopping malls found in the suburbs. Celebrate this fact by punctuating your visit to İstanbul with some exploration of the bazaars.

An Afternoon in & Around Galata (p82)

▶ Fashionable boutiques
▶ Byzantine heritage

Lying in the shadow of its medieval tower, the district of Galata melds historic credentials (intact 19th-century streetscapes and buildings, Byzantine towers and churches) with some of the city's best boutiques, a growing avant-garde arts scene, and a bustling fish market and tradesman enclave. An afternoon spent wandering here will give you glimpses into İstanbul's multifaceted lifestyle.

Weekend Wander in Ortaköy (p102)

▶ Snack and market stalls
▶ Bosphorus views

A former fishing village, Ortaköy makes the most of its magnificent Bosphorus location. Centred on a waterside square full of eateries and cafes, the suburb is home to one of the city's prettiest mosques and plays host to crowds of locals on weekends, who flock here to promenade, take ferry cruises, snack on local fast foods, browse the stalls of the Sunday handicrafts market and drink in the bars and cafes.

Ortaköy waterfront (p102)

Karaköy Fish Market (p83)

Other great places to experience the city like a local:

Hocapaşa Sokak (p51)

Kadınlar Pazarı (p66)

Galata Bridge for fish sandwiches (p68)

Mimar Sinan Teras Cafe (p70)

Manda Batmaz (p90)

Hazzo Pulo Çay Bahçesi (p92)

Türkü Evleri (p94)

Tophane Nargile Cafes (p93)

İstanbul Day Planner

Day One

With only one day, you'll need to get cracking! Head to Sultanahmet, where you can visit three of the city's top sights: the **Blue Mosque** (p28), **Aya Sofya** (p24) and the **Basilica Cistern** (p30). For lunch, join local shopkeepers enjoying traditional *hazır yemek* (ready-made dishes) at **Erol Lokantası** (p36) or **Sefa Restaurant** (p51).

Walk up Yerebatan and Nuruosmaniye Caddesis to the **Grand Bazaar** (p56). Shop, explore, drink tea and practise your bargaining skills before following our local life itinerary (p62) down the winding shopping street linking the bazaar with the bustling transport hub of Eminönü.

Cross the Galata Bridge to sample the nightlife in Beyoğlu. Kick off at a rooftop bar, such as **Mikla** (p91), then sample traditional Turkish food at **Çukur Meyhane** (p90), **Klemuri** (p88) or **Zübeyir Ocakbaşı** (p88). If you've still got energy, there are plenty of clubs and bars to keep you entertained into the early hours – current favourites are in the expat enclave of Cihangir, on the eastern edge of Taksim Meydanı (Taksim Sq), although **Babylon** (p93) in Asmalımescit is always a great choice.

Day Two

Topkapı Palace (p42) is your first destination of the day. Spend at least three hours here, being sure not to miss the Harem, Treasury and Marble Terrace, before walking down **Soğukçeşme Sokak** (p49) towards Eminönü. Stop for a simple lunch in **Hocapaşa Sokak** (p51) and a sweet treat at **Hafız Mustafa** (p52) along the way.

Take a tram and funicular to Taksim Meydanı, and walk down **İstiklal Caddesi** (p78), visiting cultural centres including **ARTER** (p79) and **SALT Beyoğlu** (p79) along the way. If you're interested in Orientalist art, make a detour to the **Pera Museum** (p86) in nearby Tepebaşı; alternatively, head to Orhan Pamuk's nostalgic **Museum of Innocence** (p87) in Çukurcuma. Then follow our local life itinerary in **Galata** (p82) and watch the sun set over the Old City from the rooftop bar at **SALT Galata** (p83).

Enjoy a drink and dinner in the hipster hotspot of Karaköy, close to the Galata Bridge – **Unter** (p92) and **Lokanta Maya** (p90) are great choices. After dinner, adjourn to **Karaköy Güllüoğlu** (p88) for a decadently rich plate of baklava, or follow the seductive scent of apple tobacco to the nargile (water pipe) cafes in **Tophane** (p93), where you are sure to encounter a colourful cast of locals.

Short on time?
We've arranged İstanbul's must-sees into these day-by-day itineraries to make sure you see the very best of the city in the time you have available.

Day Three

☀ In the morning, board the Long Bosphorus Tour (Uzun Boğaz Turu) for a one-way trip up the **Bosphorus** (p108) and then make your way back to town in the afternoon by bus, visiting museums and monuments along the way. Alternatively, spend the morning getting a background briefing on Turkish art at **İstanbul Modern** (p80) or visiting opulent **Dolmabahçe Palace** (p100).

☀ If you took the arty option in the morning, take the Dentur Avraysa hop-on/hop-off tour from Kabataş in the early afternoon and alight to visit the **Sakıp Sabancı Museum** (p110), **Küçüksu Kasrı** (p110) and **Beylerbeyi Palace** (p109).

☾ See the dervishes whirl at the **Hocapaşa Culture Centre** (p53) in Sirkeci before moving on to dinner on the rooftop of **Hamdi Restaurant** (p66) in Eminönü, a bustling place serving tasty kebaps and commanding amazing views over the city. If you've got energy to spare, head over Galata Bridge to **Nardis Jazz Club** (p94) or **Nublu İstanbul** (p94) to hear some live music.

Day Four

☀ Take the Golden Horn (Haliç) ferry from Eminönü and alight at Ayvansaray, walking uphill alongside the historic city walls to reach the **Kariye Museum** (Chora Church; p75), a repository of exquisite Byzantine mosaics and frescoes. Enjoy a lunch fit for a sultan at next-door **Asitane** (p75), which specialises in Ottoman palace cuisine.

☀ Visit the city's most magnificent imperial mosque, the **Süleymaniye** (p60), investigating its extensive *külliye* (mosque complex) buildings and pausing to have a çay and admire the panoramic view at the **Mimar Sinan Teras Cafe** (p70).

☾ Head to the Bosphorus suburbs for dinner, eating Asian at **Zuma** (p106) or **Banyan** (p106), or modern Mediterranean at **Vogue** (p106). Afterwards, party with the glitterati at one of the superclubs on the **Golden Mile** (p107).

Need to Know

For more information, see Survival Guide (p138)

Currency
Türk Lirası (Turkish Lira; ₺)

Language
Turkish

Visas
Not required for some (mainly European) nationalities; most other nationalities can obtain an electronic visa before their visit.

Money
ATMs are widely available. Credit cards are accepted at most shops, hotels and upmarket restaurants.

Mobile Phones
Most European and Australasian phones can be used here, but some North American phones can't. Check with your provider.

Time
Eastern European time (UTC/GMT plus two hours November to March; plus three hours April to October).

Plugs & Adaptors
Plugs have two round pins; electrical current is 230V. North American and Australasian visitors will require an adaptor.

Tipping
A tip of 10% is usual in most restaurants. Round taxi fares up to the nearest lira.

① Before You Go

Your Daily Budget

Budget less than €60
▶ Dorm beds €11–€25
▶ Kebap or pide dinner €6–€7
▶ Beer at a neighbourhood bar €4

Midrange €60–€200
▶ Double room from €80
▶ *Lokanta* (eatery serving ready-made food) lunch €10
▶ *Meyhane* (tavern) dinner with wine €35

Top end more than €200
▶ Double room from €200
▶ Restaurant dinner with wine €50
▶ Cocktail in a rooftop bar €12

Useful Websites

Not Only İstanbul (www.notonlyistanbul. com) Guide to the city's art, food and culture.

The Guide İstanbul (www.theguideistanbul. com) Loads of listings.

Yabangee (http://yabangee.com/) Expats' guide to the city.

Time Out İstanbul (www.timeoutistanbul. com/en/) Lots of events listings.

Lonely Planet (www.lonelyplanet.com/ istanbul) Destination information, traveller forum and more.

Advance Planning

Three months before If you're travelling in spring, autumn or over Christmas, book your hotel as far in advance as possible.

Two months before İstanbul's big-ticket festivals and concerts sell out fast; book tickets online at Biletix (www.biletix.com).

Two weeks before Ask your hotel to make dinner reservations.

② Arriving in İstanbul

Two international airports service the city: Atatürk International Airport (p140) and Sabiha Gökçen International Airport (p140). At the time of research, only one international train service – the daily *Bosfor Ekspresi* between İstanbul and Bucharest via Sofia – was operating in and out of İstanbul.

✈ From Atatürk International Airport

Destination	Best Transport
Sultanahmet	Metro & tram
Beyoğlu	Havataş Airport Bus
Bosphorus suburbs	Taxi

✈ From Sabiha Gökçen International Airport

Destination	Best Transport
Sultanahmet	Taxi
Beyoğlu	Havataş Airport Bus
Bosphorus suburbs	Taxi

✈ At the Airports

Atatürk International Airport There are ATMs, car-hire and telephone-company booths, exchange bureaux, a 24-hour pharmacy, a 24-hour supermarket, a left-luggage office and a PTT (post office) in the International Arrivals Hall. There is also a tourist information desk supplying maps.

Sabiha Gökçen International Airport There are ATMs, car-hire booking desks, exchange bureaux, a mini-market, a left-luggage office and a PTT in the International Arrivals Hall.

③ Getting Around

İstanbul has an extensive and efficient public transport system. You will save time, money and hassle by purchasing a rechargeable İstanbulkart transport card (p141).

🚋 Tram

Services run from Bağcılar to Kabataş, near Taksim Meydanı (Taskim Sq), in Beyoğlu, stopping at stations including Zeytinburnu (to connect with the airport metro), Beyazıt-Kapalı Çarşı (Grand Bazaar), Sultanahmet, and Eminönü en route. A second service runs from Cevizlibağ, closer to Sultanahmet on the same line, to Kabataş.

⛴ Ferry

Boats travel between the Asian and European shores, up and down the Golden Horn (Haliç), and along and across the Bosphorus.

🚕 Taxi

Inexpensive and plentiful.

Ⓜ Metro

The M1A connects Aksaray with the airport. The M2 connects Yenikapı with Taksim, stopping at Vezneciler near the Grand Bazaar, on the Golden Horn (Haliç) bridge and at Şişhane, near Tünel Meydanı in Beyoğlu. From Taksim another service travels northeast to Hacıosman. The Marmaray line connects Kazlıçeşme, west of the Old City, with Ayrılak Çeşmesi, on the Asian side. This travels via an underwater tunnel and stops at Yenikapı, Sirkeci and Üsküdar.

🚠 Funicular

These make the trip from the tramline up to İstiklal Caddesi in Beyoğlu easy. One connects Karaköy with Tünel; the other connects Kabataş with Taksim Meydanı.

🚌 Bus

The lines following the Bosphorus shoreline are of most interest to travellers. Be warned that trips are long and buses are crowded.

İstanbul Neighbourhoods

**Kariye Museum
(Chora Church)** 👁

İstiklal Caddesi & Beyoğlu (p76)
Dominated by İstiklal, the city's most famous boulevard, this high-octane neighbourhood hosts the best eating, drinking and entertainment options.

👁 Top Sights
İstiklal Caddesi

İstanbul Modern

İstiklal
Caddesi 👁

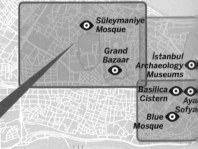

Süleymaniye
Mosque 👁

Grand
Bazaar 👁

İstanbul
Archaeology 👁
Museums

Basilica 👁 👁
Cistern   Aya
          Sofya

Blue 👁
Mosque

Grand Bazaar & the Bazaar District (p54)
A walk through this beguiling district features historic bazaars, chaotic local shopping streets and stunning imperial mosques.

👁 Top Sights
Grand Bazaar

Süleymaniye Mosque

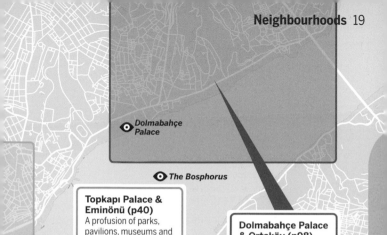

Dolmabahçe Palace

The Bosphorus

İstanbul Modern

Topkapı Palace

Topkapı Palace & Eminönü (p40)
A profusion of parks, pavilions, museums and scenic viewpoints gives this former stamping ground of the Ottoman sultans its unique allure.

⊙ Top Sights
Topkapı Palace

İstanbul Archaeology Museums

Dolmabahçe Palace & Ortaköy (p98)
Opulent Ottoman palaces and ultrafashionable nightclubs can be found along this privileged and picturesque stretch of the Bosphorus shore.

⊙ Top Sight
Dolmabahçe Palace

Aya Sofya & Sultanahmet (p22)
The famous Byzantine basilica is only one of many extraordinary museums and monuments in this ancient area.

⊙ Top Sights
Aya Sofya

Blue Mosque

Basilica Cistern

Explore
İstanbul

Worth a Trip

Twin Kiosk/Apartments of the Crown Prince (p43),
Topkapı Palace
AYHAN ALTU/GETTY IMAGES ©

Explore

Aya Sofya & Sultanahmet

Many visitors to İstanbul never make it out of Sultanahmet. And while this is a shame, it's hardly surprising. After all, its mosques and museums – including the magnificent Aya Sofya – provide a time capsule of Byzantine and Ottoman history and culture unmatched anywhere in the world, and its impressive array of sights, shops and hotels are all within easy walking distance.

The Sights in a Day

🔆 In İstanbul, all roads lead to the city's spiritual centre, Sultanahmet Park. Bookended by the grand edifices of Aya Sofya and the Blue Mosque, this unassuming garden is built over ruins of the Great Palace of Byzantium and is a good place to start your exploration of the neighbourhood. After visiting the **Blue Mosque** (p28), pop into the **Great Palace Mosaic Museum** (p33), browse the shops in the **Arasta Bazaar**, then make your way to **Aya Sofya** (p24) and the **Aya Sofya Tombs** (p33).

🔆 After lunch at **Erol Lokantası** (p36), wander through the **Hippodrome** (p33) and into the **Museum of Turkish & Islamic Arts** (p33). Afterwards, head to the **Basilica Cistern** (p30) and then relax over a sunset drink at nearby **Cihannüma** (p37) or in the rear courtyard of the **Yeşil Ev** (p37).

🌙 Sample some of the city's famous fish at **Ahırkapı Balıkçısı** (p35) or **Balıkçı Sabahattin** (p35) before winding down with a nargile (water pipe) at **Cafe Meşale** (p37) or **Derviş Aile Çay Bahçesi** (p38).

 Top Sights

Aya Sofya (p24)

Blue Mosque (p28)

Basilica Cistern (p30)

💗 Best of İstanbul

Museums
Great Palace Mosaic Museum (p33)

Museum of Turkish & Islamic Arts (p33)

Architecture
Aya Sofya (p24)

Blue Mosque (p28)

Basilica Cistern (p30)

Little Aya Sofya (p35)

Shopping
Cocoon (p38)

Jennifer's Hamam (p38)

Mehmet Çetinkaya Gallery (p39)

Tulu (p39)

Getting There

🚋 **Tram** Trams run between Bağcılar and Cevizlibağ on the western side of the Old City to Kabataş near Taksim Meydanı (Taksim Sq) in Beyoğlu. Alight at the Sultanahmet stop.

Top Sights
Aya Sofya

There are many important monuments in İstanbul, but this venerable structure – commissioned by Emperor Justinian and consecrated as a church in 537, converted to a mosque by Mehmet the Conqueror in 1453 and declared a museum by Atatürk in 1934 – surpasses the rest due to its rich history, religious importance and extraordinary beauty. Known as Hagia Sophia in Greek, Sancta Sophia in Latin and the Church of the Divine Wisdom in English, it is commonly acknowledged as one of the world's greatest buildings.

👁 Map p18, D1

www.ayasofyamuzesi.gov.tr

Aya Sofya Meydanı 1

adult/child under 12yr ₺30/free

🕙9am-6pm Tue-Sun mid-Apr–Sep, to 4pm Oct–mid-Apr

🚊Sultanahmet

Don't Miss

Imperial Door

The main entrance into the nave is crowned with a mosaic of Christ as Pantocrator (Ruler of All). Christ holds a book that carries the inscription 'Peace be with you. I am the Light of the World' and is flanked by the Virgin Mary and the Archangel Gabriel. At his feet an emperor (probably Leo VI) prostrates himself.

Nave

Made 'transparent' by its lack of obtrusive supporting columns, Aya Sofya's nave is as visually arresting as it is enormous. The chandeliers hanging low above the floor are Ottoman additions, as are the 19th-century medallions inscribed with gilt Arabic letters and the elevated kiosk where the sultan worshipped.

Apse

The 9th-century mosaic of the Virgin and Christ Child in the apse is the focal point of the nave. A *mimber* (pulpit) and *mihrab* (prayer niche indicating the direction of Mecca) were added by the Ottomans.

Dome

The famous dome measures 30m in diameter and 56m in height. It is supported by 40 massive ribs resting on four huge pillars concealed in the interior walls. On its completion, the Byzantine historian Procopius described it as being 'hung from heaven on a golden chain'.

Seraphs

The four huge winged angels at the base of the dome were originally mosaic, but two (on the western side) were re-created as frescoes after being damaged in the 13th century. All four faces

---

☑ Top Tips

▶ The museum is at its busiest first thing in the morning and midafternoon, when tour groups descend en masse. Visit during lunchtime or late in the day to avoid the crowds and long ticket queue.

▶ Bypass the ticket queue by pre-purchasing a Museum Pass İstanbul.

▶ Bring binoculars if you want to properly view the mosaic portraits in the apse and under the dome.

▶ Visit the nave first (entering through the Imperial Door), followed by the upstairs galleries.

✗ Take a Break

Retreat to the tranquil courtyard at the nearby Yeşil Ev hotel (p37) to escape the crowds and enjoy a drink or light lunch.

Piping hot pides (Turkish pizzas) are on offer at Karadeniz Aile Pide ve Kebap Salonu (p36), just off Divan Yolu.

were covered by metallic discs during the Ottoman period, and are slowly being restored. One was unveiled in 2009.

Saints Mosaics

When in the nave, look up towards the northeast (to your left if you are facing the apse), and you will see three mosaics at the base of the northern tympanum (semicircle) beneath the dome. These are 9th-century portraits of St Ignatius the Younger, St John Chrysostom and St Ignatius Theodorus of Antioch. Next to them (but only visible from the upstairs north gallery) is a mosaic portrait of Emperor Alexandros.

Weeping Column

Legend has it that this column in the northeast aisle was blessed by St Gregory the Miracle Worker and that putting one's finger into its hole can lead to the healing of ailments if the finger emerges moist.

Upstairs Galleries

To access the galleries, walk up the switchback ramp at the northern end of the inner narthex. When you reach the top you'll find a large circle of green marble marking the spot where the throne of the empress once stood. The view over the main space towards the apse from this vantage point is quite spectacular.

Aya Sofya – Ground Floor & Upstairs Galleries

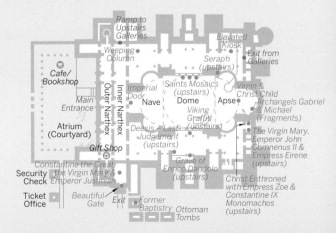

Deesis (Last Judgement)

The remnants of this magnificent 13th-century mosaic are in the up-stairs south gallery. It depicts Christ with the Virgin Mary on his left and John the Baptist on his right.

Grave of Enrico Dandolo

Dandolo, who was Doge of Venice, led the soldiers of the Fourth Crusade who conquered Constantinople in 1204. He died in the city the following year, and was buried in Aya Sofya's upper gallery. A 19th-century marker indicates the probable location of his grave.

Christ Enthroned with Empress Zoe & Constantine IX Monomachos

This mosaic portrait in the upper gallery depicts Zoe (r 1042), one of only three Byzantine women to rule as empress in their own right.

The Virgin Mary, Emperor John Comnenus II & Empress Eirene

A wonderful mosaic featuring 'John the Good' on the Virgin's left and his wife Eirene, who was known for her charitable works, on the Virgin's right. Their son Alexius, who died soon after the portrait was made, is depicted next to Eirene.

Viking Graffiti

Graffiti dating from the 9th century is carved into a marble banister in the upstairs south balcony. It is thought to have been the work of a mercenary called Halvdan.

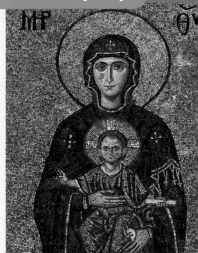

Mosaic of the Virgin and Christ Child (p25)

Constantine the Great, the Virgin Mary & Emperor Justinian

As you exit the building, don't miss this 10th-century mosaic showing Constantine (right) offering the Virgin Mary the city of Constantinople; Justinian (left) is offering her Hagia Sophia.

Ottoman Tombs

The beautifully decorated tombs (p33) of five Ottoman sultans and their families are located in Aya Sofya's southern corner and accessed via Kabasakal Caddesi. One of the tombs occupies the original church's Baptistry.

Top Sights
Blue Mosque

İstanbul's most photogenic building was the grand project of Sultan Ahmet I (r 1603–17), whose *türbe* (tomb) is located on the northern side of the site facing Sultanahmet Park and Aya Sofya. The mosque's wonderfully curvaceous exterior features a huge courtyard, a cascade of domes and six slender minarets (more than any other Ottoman mosque). Inside, thousands of blue İznik tiles adorn the walls and give the building its unofficial but commonly used name.

Sultanahmet Camii

◉ Map p18, C3

Hippodrome

⊙ closed to tourists during the 5 daily prayer times & Fri sermon

🚊 Sultanahmet

Don't Miss

The Ceremonial Entrance

The mosque is best approached via the Hippodrome. When entering the courtyard, you'll be able to appreciate the perfect proportions of the building and see how a progression of domes draws worshippers' eyes from ground level (ie earth) to the dome and minarets (ie heaven).

Prayer Hall

The 260 stained-glass windows and mass of İznik tiles immediately attract attention, and the dome and semidomes are painted with graceful arabesques. Notable structures include an elevated kiosk covered with marble latticework; a *mihrab* featuring a piece of the sacred Black Stone from the Kaaba in Mecca; a high *mahfil* (chair) from which the imam gives the sermon on Fridays; and a beautifully carved white marble *mimber*.

The Mosque Complex

Imperial mosques usually incorporated public-service institutions such as hospitals, soup kitchens and hamams. Here, a large *medrese* (Islamic school of higher studies; closed to the public) and *arasta* (row of shops by a mosque; now the **Arasta Bazaar**) remain. The rent from shops in the *arasta* has traditionally supported the upkeep of the mosque; the best shopping in Sultanahmet is found in and around this historic arcade.

Tomb of Sultan Ahmet I

Ahmet died one year after his mosque was constructed, aged only 27. Buried with him are his wife, Kösem, who was strangled to death in the Topkapı Harem, and his sons, Sultan Osman II, Sultan Murat IV and Prince Beyazıt (strangled by order of Murat). Like the mosque, the tomb features fine İznik tiles.

☑ Top Tips

▶ Only worshippers are admitted through the main eastern door; tourists must use the southern door (follow the signs).

▶ Women should bring a shawl to cover their heads and shoulders; those without one will be loaned a headscarf or chador.

▶ Shoes must be removed before entering the prayer hall; it's best to carry them with you in a plastic bag (provided) rather than leaving them on the shelves.

✗ Take a Break

The leafy Derviş Aile Çay Bahçesi (p38) opposite the mosque is a good spot for tea, fresh juice and people-watching.

For simple but tasty Anatolian dishes served in pleasant modern surrounds, head to nearby Cooking Alaturka (p35).

Top Sights
Basilica Cistern

Commissioned by Emperor Justinian, this subterranean structure was built in 532 beneath the Stoa Basilica, a great square that occupied Byzantium's First Hill. The largest surviving Byzantine cistern in İstanbul, it features a forest of 336 marble and granite columns, many of which were salvaged from ruined classical temples and have fine carved capitals. The cistern's symmetry and sheer grandeur of conception are quite breathtaking, making it a favourite location for big-budget films (remember *From Russia With Love*?).

Yerebatan Sarnıçı

⊙ Map p18, C1

www.yerebatan.com

Yerebatan Caddesi 13

⊙9am-6.30pm mid-Apr–Sep, till 5.30pm Nov–mid-Apr

Sultanahmet

Medusa head

Don't Miss

Columns

The cistern's columns are all 9m high; most have Ionic or Corinthian capitals. Arranged in 12 rows, they include one column which has been engraved with shapes that are often described as peacock's eyes, or tears. Some historians assert that these tears were carved to pay tribute to the hundreds of slaves who died during the construction of the cistern.

Medusa Heads

Two columns feature striking bases carved with the head of Medusa. One is upside down, the other on its side. When the building functioned as a cistern, both would have lain beneath the surface of the water. Now revealed, they provide the building with an element of mystery.

The Fish

The cistern was built to store water for the Great Palace of Byzantium, a sprawling complex occupying the area between the Hippodrome and the Sea of Marmara. After the Conquest, it supplied water to irrigate the gardens of Topkapı Palace. Decommissioned in the 19th century, its shallow water is now home to ghostly patrols of carp and goldfish that can be seen from the cistern's elevated wooden walkways.

☑ Top Tips

▶ The cistern is a blissfully cool retreat on hot summer days – visit in the afternoon, when the city's heat can be particularly oppressive.

▶ Watch young children carefully, as the walkways over the water don't have much of a safety barrier.

▶ Admission is officially ₺20 for foreigners but in reality ₺10.

✕ Take a Break

Hafız Mustafa (p36) is a good spot to enjoy a glass of tea and sweet treats such as *lokum* (Turkish delight) and *fırın sutlaç* (rice pudding).

For a cheap and tasty lunch, head to Erol Lokantası (p36), a popular *lokanta* (eatery serving ready-made food) – try to arrive at the start of service, as dishes can sell out quickly.

200 m
0.1 miles

Sea of Marmara

Ahırkapı İskelesi (Ferry Dock)

Kennedy Cad (Sahil Yolu)

İshakpaşa Cad

CANKURTARAN

Aya Sofya Tombs

Aya Sofya

Basilica Cistern

Alemdar Cad

Aya Sofya Meydanı

SULTANAHMET

Sultanahmet Park

Blue Mosque

Great Palace Mosaic Museum

ALEMDAR

BINBIRDIREK

Museum of Turkish & Islamic Arts

Hippodrome

Divan Yolu (Ordu) Cad

KÜÇÜK AYASOFYA

Little Aya Sofya

Sights

Museum of Turkish & Islamic Arts
MUSEUM

 Map p32, B2

This Ottoman palace on the western edge of the Hippodrome was built in 1524 for İbrahim Paşa, childhood friend, brother-in-law and grand vizier of Süleyman the Magnificent. Undergoing a major renovation at the time of research, it has a magnificent collection of artefacts, including exquisite examples of calligraphy and one of the world's most impressive collections of antique carpets. (Türk ve İslam Eserleri Müzesi; www.tiem.gov.tr; Atmeydanı Caddesi 46; adult/child under 12yr ₺20/free; ⏰refer to website; 🚊Sultanahmet)

Hippodrome
PARK

 Map p32, B2

The Byzantine Emperors loved nothing more than an afternoon at the chariot races, and this rectangular arena was their venue of choice. In its heyday, it was decorated by obelisks and statues, some of which remain in place today. Recently re-landscaped, it is one of the city's most popular meeting places and promenades. (Atmeydanı; 🚊Sultanahmet)

Aya Sofya Tombs
TOMBS

 Map p32, D2

Part of the Aya Sofya complex but entered via Kabasakal Caddesi, these tombs are the final resting places of

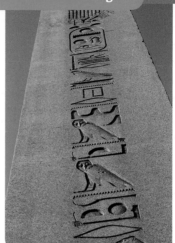

Obelisk in the Hippodrome

five sultans – Mehmed III, Selim II, Murad III, İbrahim I and Mustafa I – most of whom are buried with members of their families. The ornate interior decoration in the tombs features the very best Ottoman tilework, calligraphy and decorative paintwork. (Aya Sofya Müzesi Padişah Türbeleri; Kabasakal Caddesi; admission free; ⏰9am-5pm; 🚊Sultanahmet)

Great Palace Mosaic Museum
MUSEUM

 Map p32, C3

When archaeologists from the University of Ankara and the University of St Andrews (Scotland) excavated around the Arasta Bazaar at the rear of the Blue Mosque in the 1930s and

Understand

Byzantium

Known for its charismatic emperors, powerful armies, refined culture and convoluted politics, Byzantium's legacy resonates to this day.

The Eastern Roman Empire

Legend tells us that the city of Byzantium was founded in 667 BC by a group of colonists from Megara, northwest of Athens, led by Byzas, the son of Megara's king. An alliance was eventually formed with the Romans, and the city was officially incorporated into their empire in AD 79. In the late 3rd century, Emperor Diocletian (r 284–305) split the empire into eastern and western administrative units. His actions resulted in a civil war in which a rival, Constantine I, triumphed. Constantine made Byzantium his capital in 330, naming it 'New Rome'.

The new capital soon came to be known as Constantinople. Constantine died in 337, but the city continued to grow under the rule of emperors including Theodosius I ('the Great'; r 379–95), Theodosius II (r 408–50) and Justinian (r 527–65). The eastern and western empires had been politically separated after the death of Theodosius I, but the final tie with Rome wasn't severed until 620, when Heraclius I (r 610–41) changed the official language of the eastern empire from Latin to Greek, inaugurating what we now refer to as 'The Byzantine Empire'.

The Byzantine Empire

For the next eight centuries the empire asserted its independence from Rome by adopting Orthodox Christianity. Ruled by a series of family dynasties, it was the most powerful economic, cultural and military force in Europe until the Seljuk Turks acquired much of its territory in Asia Minor in 1071.

In 1204 Constantinople fell to Latin soldiers of the Fourth Crusade. The powerful Byzantine families went into exile in Nicaea and Epirus, and the empire was split between Greek and Latin factions. Despite being reclaimed by the Nicaean emperor Michael VIII Palaiologos in 1261, it was plagued by a series of civil wars and finally fell to the Ottomans in 1453, when Mehmet II (Fatih, or Conqueror) took Constantinople. The last Byzantine emperor, Constantine XI Palaiologos, died defending the walls from Mehmet's onslaught.

1950s, they uncovered a stunning mosaic pavement featuring hunting and mythological scenes. Dating from early Byzantine times, it was restored between 1983 and 1997 and is now preserved in this museum. (☎212-518 1205; Torun Sokak; admission ₺10; ☺9am-5.30pm Tue-Sun mid-Apr–Sep, to 3.30pm Oct–mid-Apr; 🚊Sultanahmet)

Little Aya Sofya   MOSQUE

 5   Map p32, A4

Justinian and his wife Theodora built this little church sometime between 527 and 536, just before Justinian built Aya Sofya. You can still see their monogram worked into some of the frilly white capitals. The building is one of the most beautiful Byzantine structures in the city despite being thoroughly transformed into a mosque during a recent restoration. (Küçük Aya Sofya Camii, SS Sergius & Bacchus Church; Küçük Ayasofya Caddesi; admission free; 🚊Sultanahmet or Çemberlitaş)

Eating

Balıkçı Sabahattin   FISH €€€

 6   Map p32, D3

The limos outside Balıkçı Sabahattin pay testament to its enduring popularity with the city's establishment, who join cashed-up tourists in enjoying its limited menu of meze and fish. The food here is the best in Sultanahmet, though the service is often harried. You'll dine under a leafy canopy in the garden (one section smoking, the other nonsmoking). (☎212-458 1824; www.balikcisabahattin.com; Şeyit Hasan Koyu Sokak 1, Cankurtaran; mezes ₺10-30, fish ₺30-65; ☺noon-midnight; 🚊Sultanahmet)

Cooking Alaturka   TURKISH €€

 7   Map p32, D3

Dutch-born owner/chef Eveline Zoutendijk and her Turkish colleague Fehzi Yıldırım serve a set four-course menu of simple Anatolian dishes at this hybrid cooking school-restaurant near the Blue Mosque. The menu makes the most of fresh seasonal produce, and can be tailored to suit vegetarians or those with food allergies (call ahead). No children under six years at dinner and no credit cards. (☎212-458 5919; www.cookingalaturka.com; Akbıyık Caddesi 72a, Cankurtaran; set lunch or dinner ₺55; ☺lunch Mon-Sat & dinner by reservation Mon-Sat; 🍴; 🚊Sultanahmet)

Ahırkapı Balıkçısı   SEAFOOD €€

8   Map p32, D4

For years we promised locals that we wouldn't review this neighbourhood fish restaurant. We sympathised with their desire to retain the place's low profile, particularly as it's tiny and authentically Turkish. However, other decent options are so scarce on the ground that we've finally decided to share the secret. Get here early to score a table. (☎212-518 4988; Keresteci Hakkı Sokak 46, Cankurtaran; meze ₺5-30, fish ₺30-50; ☺5.30-10pm; 🚊Sultanahmet)

Erol Lokantası
TURKISH €

9 ✗ Map p32, B1

One of the last *lokantas* (eateries serving ready-made food) in Sultanahmet, Erol wouldn't win any awards for its interior design but might for its food – the dishes in the bain marie are made fresh each day using seasonal ingredients and are really very good. Opt for a meat or vegetable stew served with buttery pilaf. (☎212-511 0322; Çatal Çeşme Sokak 3, Cağaloğlu; portions ₺6-14; ⏰11am-9pm Mon-Sat; 🖍; 🚃Sultanahmet)

Karadeniz Aile Pide ve Kebap Salonu
PIDE, KEBAP €

10 ✗ Map p32, B1

The original Karadeniz (Black Sea) style pide joint in this enclave off Divan Yolu, this popular place serves tasty pides and kebaps and is very popular with local shopkeepers. You can claim a table in the utilitarian interior (women usually sit upstairs) or on the cobbled lane. No alcohol. (☎212-528 6290; www.karadenizpide.net; Hacı Tahsinbey Sokak 7, off Divan Yolu Caddesi; pides ₺12-17, kebaps ₺14-24; ⏰11am-11pm; 🚃Sultanahmet)

Sofa Cafe Restaurant
RESTAURANT, BAR €

11 ✗ Map p32, D3

Ten candlelit tables beckon patrons into this friendly cafe-bar just off Akbıyık Caddesi. There's a happy hour (in fact three) between 3.30pm and 6.30pm each day and a decidedly laid-back feel. The food is cheap but tasty, the glasses of wine are generous and the Efes is cold, meaning that there's plenty to like. (☎212-458 3630; Mimar Mehmet Ağa Caddesi 32, Cankurtaran; burgers ₺14, pastas ₺15-20, Turkish mains ₺17-35; ⏰11am-11pm; 🚃Sultanahmet)

Hafız Mustafa
SWEETS €

12 ✗ Map p32, C1

Located in the Kıraathanesi Foundation of Turkish Literature, this branch of one of the city's most popular *şekerleme* (sweets shops) is a great place for a mid-morning or mid-afternoon pit stop. (☎212-514 9068; Divan Yolu Caddesi 14, Sultanahmet; ⏰9am-midnight; 🚃Sultanahmet)

Understand
Naming Rights

The name İstanbul probably derives from *'eis ten polin'* (Greek for 'to the city'). Though the Turks kept the name Constantinople after the Conquest, they also used other names, including İstanbul and Dersaadet (City of Peace and/or Happiness). The city's name was officially changed to İstanbul by Atatürk in the early republican years.

Pides (Turkish pizzas)

Drinking

Cihannüma
BAR, RESTAURANT

13 Map p32, C1

We don't recommend eating at the restaurant on the top-floor of this hotel near Aya Sofya, but the view from its narrow balcony and glass-sheathed dining room is one of the best in the Old City (Aya Sofya, Blue Mosque, Topkapı Palace, Galata Tower and Bosphorus Bridge), so it's a great choice for a late-afternoon coffee or sunset drink. (☑212-520 7676; www.cihannumaistanbul.com; And Hotel, Yerebatan Caddesi 18; ⏰noon-midnight; 🚇Sultanahmet)

Yeşil Ev
BAR

14 Map p32, D2

The elegant rear courtyard of this Ottoman-style hotel is a true oasis for those wanting to enjoy a quiet drink. In spring, flowers and blossoms fill every corner; in summer, the fountain and trees keep the temperature down. You can order a sandwich, salad or cheese platter if you're peckish. (Kabasakal Caddesi 5; ⏰noon-10.30pm; 🚇Sultanahmet)

Cafe Meşale
NARGILE CAFE

15 Map p32, C3

Located in a sunken courtyard behind the Blue Mosque, Meşale is a tourist

Traditional ceramics for sale

trap *par excellence,* but still has loads of charm. Generations of backpackers have joined locals in claiming one of its cushioned benches and enjoying a tea and nargile. It has sporadic live Turkish music and a bustling vibe in the evening. (Arasta Bazaar, Utangaç Sokak, Cankurtaran; ☺24hr; 🚊Sultanahmet)

Derviş Aile Çay Bahçesi
TEA GARDEN

16 Map p32, C2

Superbly located directly opposite the Blue Mosque, the Derviş beckons patrons with its comfortable cane chairs and shady trees. Efficient service, reasonable prices and peerless people-watching opportunities make it a

great place for a leisurely tea, nargile and game of backgammon. (Mimar Mehmet Ağa Caddesi; ☺7am-midnight Apr-Oct; 🚊Sultanahmet)

Shopping

Cocoon
CARPETS, TEXTILES

17 Map p32, C4

There are so many rug and textile shops in İstanbul that choosing individual businesses to recommend is incredibly difficult. We had no problem whatsoever in singling this one out, though. Felt hats, felt-and-silk scarves and textiles from central Asia are artfully displayed in one store, while rugs from Persia, Central Asia, the Caucasus and Anatolia adorn the other. (📞212-638 6271; www.cocoontr.com; Küçük Ayasofya Caddesi 15 & 19; ☺9am-6pm; 🚊Sultanahmet)

Jennifer's Hamam
BATHWARE

18 Map p32, C3

Owned by Canadian Jennifer Gaudet, this shop stocks top-quality hamam items including towels, robes and *peştemals* (bath wraps) produced using certified organic cotton on old-style shuttled looms. It also sells natural soaps and *keses* (coarse cloth mittens used for exfoliation). Prices are set, with no bargaining. (📞212-518 0648; www.jennifershamam.com; 135 Arasta Bazaar; ☺9am-9pm Apr-Oct, 9am-7pm Nov-Mar; 🚊Sultanahmet)

Mehmet Çetinkaya Gallery
CARPETS, TEXTILES

19 🔒 Map p32, C4

Mehmet Çetinkaya is known as one of the country's foremost experts on antique oriental carpets and kilims (woven rugs). His flagship store-cum-gallery stocks items that have artistic and ethnographic significance, and is full of treasures. There's a second shop selling rugs, textiles and objects in the Arasta Bazaar. (📞212-517 6808; www.cetinkayagallery.com; Tavukhane Sokak 7; ⏰9.30am-7.30pm; 🚋Sultanahmet)

Khaftan
ART, ANTIQUES

20 🔒 Map p32, B3

Gleaming Russian icons, delicate calligraphy (old and new), ceramics, Karagöz puppets and contemporary paintings are all on show in this attractive shop on the hill beneath the Hippodrome. (Nakilbent Sokak 33; ⏰9am-6.30pm; 🚋Sultanahmet)

İznik Classics
CERAMICS

21 🔒 Map p32, D3

İznik Classics is one of the best places in town to source hand-painted collector-item ceramics made with real quartz and using metal oxides for pigments. Admire the range here or at the other branches at Arasta Bazaar and in the Grand Bazaar. (📞212-516 8874; www.iznikclassics.com; 13-17 Utangaç Sokak; ⏰9am-8pm; 🚋Sultanahmet)

Tulu
HOMEWARES

22 🔒 Map p32, B3

One of the new breed of contemporary homeware stores in İstanbul, Tulu is owned by American Elizabeth Hewitt, a textile collector and designer who produces a stylish range of cushions, bedding and accessories inspired by textiles from Central Asia. These are sold alongside an array of furniture, textiles and objects sourced in countries including Uzbekistan, India, Japan and Indonesia. (📞212-518 8710; www.tulutextiles.com; Üçler Sokak 7; 🚋Sultanahmet)

Yilmaz Ipekçilik
TEXTILES

23 🔒 Map p32, E3

Well-priced hand-loomed silk textiles made in Antakya are on sale in this slightly out-of-the-way shop. Family-run, the business has been operating since 1950 and specialises in producing good-quality scarves, shawls and *peştemals*. (📞212-638 4579; www.yilmazipekcilik.com/en; İshakpaşa Caddesi 36; ⏰9am-9pm Mon-Sat, to 7pm winter; 🚋Sultanahmet)

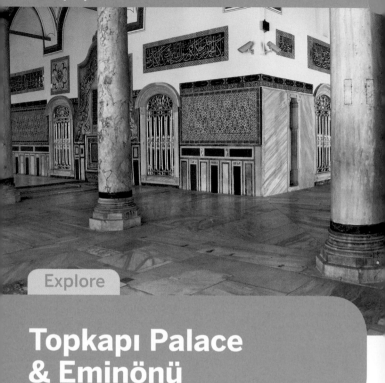

Explore

Topkapı Palace & Eminönü

The leafy parks and gardens in and around the opulent Ottoman Topkapı Palace stand in stark contrast to the crowded shopping streets clustered around the Eminönü ferry docks, but both areas are full of life and well worth a visit. Topkapı ıs perennially packed with tourists and Eminönü with locals; between them lies Gülhane Park, a tranquil retreat popular with both groups.

The Sights in a Day

☀ **Topkapı Palace** (p42) is one of Turkey's most compelling cultural attractions so you'll need a full half-day to do it justice; start early to make the most of your time. After exploring all four courtyards of this historically significant landmark, make sure you detour into **Soğukçeşme Sokak** (p49) to admire one of the city's prettiest streetscapes and visit the recently opened **Carpet Museum** (p49).

☀ After joining the locals for lunch at one of the eateries on Hocapaşa Sokak, backtrack to the **İstanbul Archaeology Museums** (p46), home to the palace collections acquired by the sultans. Afterwards, enjoy the tea and panoramic view on offer at **Set Üstü Çay Bahçesi** (p52) in **Gülhane Park** (p49), then head to Eminönü to stock up on *lokum* (Turkish delight) at one of the city's oldest shops, **Ali Muhiddin Hacı Bekir** (p53).

☽ Watch dervishes whirl at the **Hocapaşa Culture Centre** (p53) and then make your way back to the palace district to enjoy an Ottoman dinner fit for a sultan at **Matbah** (p51).

◉ Top Sights

Topkapı Palace (p42)

İstanbul Archaeology Museums (p46)

♥ Best of İstanbul

Eating

Matbah (p51)

Şehzade Cağ Kebabı (p51)

Shopping

Özlem Tuna (p53)

Ali Muhiddin Hacı Bekir (p53)

Getting There

🚋 **Tram** Trams run between Bağcılar and Cevizlibağ on the western side of the Old City and Kabataş near Taksim Meydanı (Taksim Sq) in Beyoğlu, stopping at Sultanahmet, Gülhane and Sirkeci en route.

Top Sights
Topkapı Palace

Topkapı is the subject of more colourful stories than most of the world's museums put together. Libidinous sultans, ambitious courtiers, beautiful concubines and scheming eunuchs lived and worked here between the 15th and 19th centuries when the palace was the seat of the Ottoman sultanate. Visiting its opulent pavilions, landscaped courtyards, jewel-filled Treasury and sprawling Harem gives a fascinating glimpse into the lives of the sultans and their families, as well as offering an insight into the history and customs of a once mighty empire.

◉ Map p18, D3

www.topkapisarayi.gov.tr

Babıhümayun Caddesi

palace admission adult/ child under 12yr ₺30/free

⊘9am–6pm Wed–Mon mid-Apr–Oct, to 4pm Nov–mid-Apr

🚊Sultanahmet

The Imperial Hall in the Harem

Don't Miss

First Court

Before you enter the Imperial Gate (Bab-ı Hümayun), pause to view the gorgeous rococo-style **Fountain of Sultan Ahmet III** in the middle of the cobbled roundabout. Passing through the gate, you will enter the Court of the Janissaries, also known as the First Court. On your left is the Byzantine church of Hagia Eirene, more commonly known as Aya İrini (p49).

Second Court

The second of the palace's huge courtyards is home to audience pavilions, barracks, kitchens and sleeping quarters. Be sure to visit the Outer Treasury, where an impressive collection of Ottoman and European armour is displayed.

Imperial Council Chamber

This ornate chamber on the left (west) side of the Second Court is where the Imperial Divân (Council) made laws, where citizens presented petitions and where foreign dignitaries were presented to the court. The sultan eavesdropped on proceedings through the gold grille high in the wall.

Harem

This complex on the western side of the Second Court was the private quarters of the sultans and their families. It features many opulently decorated bed chambers, reception rooms, hamams and courtyards. Highlights include the Salon of the Valide, Imperial Hall, Privy Chamber of Murat III, Privy Chamber of Ahmet III and Twin Kiosk/Apartments of the Crown Prince.

Third Court

The Third Court is entered through the impressive **Gate of Felicity**, a rococo-style structure that was

---

☑ Top Tips

▶ If you decide to visit the Harem – and we highly recommend that you do – you'll need to buy a dedicated ticket from the main ticket office.

▶ Be sure to admire the spectacular views from the terrace above the Konyalı Restaurant and from the Marble Terrace in the Fourth Court.

▶ Topkapı Palace can be accessed from both the Gülhane and Sultanahmet tram stops, but note that it's a steep uphill walk from Gülhane.

✗ Take a Break

There are wonderful views from many of the terrace tables in the palace's Konyalı Restaurant, but the quality of food leaves a lot to be desired.

In sunny weather, the courtyard of the Caferağa Medresesi Çay Bahçesi (p53), built in 1560 by order of Cafer Ağa, Süleyman the Magnificent's chief black eunuch, is a great place to enjoy a çay.

Topkapı Palace

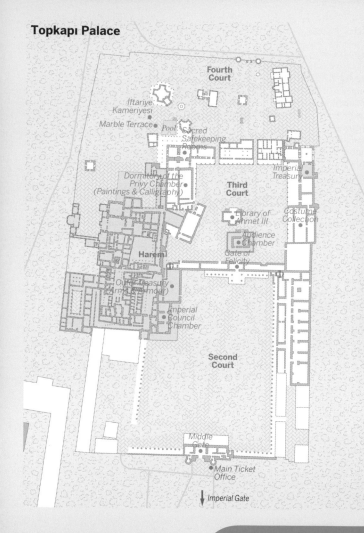

Fourth Court

Iftariye
Kameriyesi

Marble Terrace • Pool

Sacred
Safekeeping
Rooms

Imperial
Treasury

Dormitory of the
Privy Chamber
(Paintings & Calligraphy)

Third Court

Library of
Ahmet III

Costume
Collection

Audience
Chamber

Gate of
Felicity

Harem

Outer Treasury
(Arms & Armour)

Imperial
Council
Chamber

Second Court

Middle
Gate

• Main Ticket
Office

↓ Imperial Gate

used for state ceremonies including the sultan's accession and funeral. Behind it was the sultan's private domain, staffed and guarded by eunuchs.

Audience Chamber

Important officials and foreign ambassadors were brought to this pavilion for imperial audiences. The sultan, seated on cushions embroidered with hundreds of seed pearls, inspected the ambassadors' gifts and offerings as they were passed through the small doorway on the left.

Library of Ahmet III

Directly behind the Audience Chamber is this pretty library, built in 1719 for Sultan Ahmet III. Light-filled, it has comfortable reading areas and stunning inlaid woodwork.

Costume Collection

On the eastern edge of the Third Court is the Dormitory of the Expeditionary Force, which now houses a rich collection of imperial robes, kaftans and uniforms worked in silver and gold thread. Also here is a fascinating collection of talismanic shirts, which were believed to protect the wearer from enemies and misfortunes.

Sacred Safekeeping Rooms

Sumptuously decorated with İznik tiles, these rooms are a repository for many sacred relics. When the sultans lived here, the rooms were only opened once a year on the 15th day of the holy month of Ramazan.

Dormitory of the Privy Chamber

This dormitory next to the Sacred Safekeeping Rooms now houses portraits of 36 sultans. It includes a wonderful painting of the *Enthronment Ceremony of Sultan Selim III* (1789) by court painter Kostantin Kapidagi.

Imperial Treasury

The Treasury's most famous exhibit is the Topkapı Dagger, which features three enormous emeralds on its hilt. Also here is the Kaşıkçı (Spoonmaker's) Diamond, a teardrop-shaped 86-carat rock surrounded by dozens of smaller stones. First worn by Mehmet IV at his accession to the throne in 1648, it's one of the largest diamonds in the world.

Marble Terrace

This gorgeous terrace in the Fourth Court is home to the Baghdad and Revan Kiosks, wonderful examples of classical palace architecture built in 1636 and 1639 respectively. The smaller Sünnet Odası (Circumcision Room) dates from 1640 and has outer walls covered with particularly beautiful İznik tiles.

İftariye Kameriyesi

During Ramazan, the sultans would enjoy their *iftar* (breaking of the fast) under this gilded canopy overlooking the Bosphorus and Golden Horn (Haliç). These days it's a popular location for happy snaps.

Top Sights
İstanbul Archaeology Museums

This superb museum complex houses archaeological and artistic treasures from the Imperial collections. Housed in three historic buildings, its exhibits include ancient artefacts, classical statuary and objects showcasing Anatolian history. Though there are many highlights, history buffs will find the *İstanbul Through the Ages* exhibition particularly satisfying, and admirers of classical art will be blown away by the carved sarcophagi from the Royal Necropolis of Sidon.

İstanbul Arkeoloji Müzeleri

◉ Map p18, C3

www.istanbularkeoloji.gov.tr

Osman Hamdi Bey Yokuşu

adult/under 12yr ₺15/free

⏱9am-6pm Tue-Sun mid-Apr–Sep, to 4pm Oct–mid-Apr

🚋Gülhane

Don't Miss

Archaeology Museum
This imposing neoclassical building is the heart of the museum complex. It houses an extensive collection of classical statuary and sarcophagi, including the extraordinary **Alexander Sarcophagus**, carved out of Pentelic marble and dating from the last quarter of the 4th century BC.

The Columned Sarcophagi of Anatolia
Amazingly detailed sarcophagi dating from between AD 140 and 270 feature in this exhibit. Many look like tiny temples or residential buildings; don't miss the **Sidamara Sarcophagus** from Konya.

İstanbul Through the Ages
Tracing the city's history using objects and interpretive panels, this fascinating albeit dusty exhibition on the upstairs level of the Archaeology Museum traces the city's history through its neighbourhoods during different periods: Archaic, Hellenistic, Roman, Byzantine and Ottoman.

Museum of the Ancient Orient
To your immediate left as you enter the complex, this 1883 building showcases a collection of pre-Islamic items collected from the expanse of the Ottoman Empire. Highlights include a series of large blue-and-yellow glazed-brick panels that once lined the processional street and the Ishtar Gate of ancient Babylon.

Tiled Pavilion
Built in 1472 as part of the Topkapı complex, this pavilion was originally used for watching sporting events but now houses an impressive collection of Seljuk, Anatolian and Ottoman tiles.

☑ Top Tips

▶ Unless you have a particular interest in the subject areas, the *Anatolia and Troy Through the Ages* and *Neighbouring Cultures of Anatolia, Cyprus, Syria and Palestine* exhibitions on the upper floors of the Archaeology Museum can easily be given a miss.

▶ If possible, visit the museum and Topkapı Palace on separate days – jamming them into a one-day itinerary may result in museum meltdown.

✗ Take a Break

After spending a few hours admiring the collectios, enjoy panoramic views and a pot of tea at the Set Üstü Çay Bahçesi (p52), a terraced tea garden in nearby Gülhane Park.

To lunch alongside locals, head to atmospheric Hocapaşa Sokak in Sirkeci, which is full of cheap eateries.

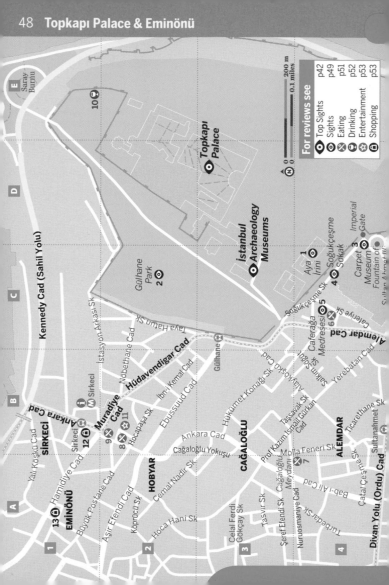

Saray
Burnu

Kennedy Cad (Sahil Yolu)

For reviews see

	Top Sights	p42
	Sights	p49
	Eating	p51
	Drinking	p52
	Entertainment	p53
	Shopping	p53

200 m
0.1 miles

10

Topkapı
Palace

Gülhane
Park 2

İstanbul
Archaeology
Museums

Aya 1
İrini

Soğukçeşme
Sokak

Carpet 3
Museum

Imperial
Gate

Fountain of
Sultan Ahmet III

Soğukçeşme Sk

5

Caferağa
Medresesi 6

Galeriye Sk

Caferiye Sk

Alemdar Cad

Yerebatan Cad

SİRKECİ

Ankara Cad

Sirkeci

Sirkeci

EMİNÖNÜ

13

Hamidiye Cad

Yalı Köşkü Cad

Muradiye
Cad

Hüdavendigar Cad

Nöbethane Cad

İstasyon Arkası Sk

Taya Hatun Sk

İbn-i Kemal Cad

Ebussuud Cad

Gülhane Cad

Alayköşkü Cad

Hükümet Konağı Sk

Salkım Söğüt Sk

9

8

11

Hocapaşa Sk

Ankara Cad

Cağaloğlu Yokuşu

HOBYAR

Cemal Nadir Sk

Büyük Postane Cad

Aşır Efendi Cad

Köprücü Sk

Hoca Hani Sk

Celal Ferdi
Gökçay Sk

Taşvir Sk

CAĞALOĞLU

Tassavak Sk

Prof Kazım İsmail Gürkan
Cad

Cağaloğlu
Meydanı

Molla Feneri Sk

Ticarethane Sk

ALEMDAR

Çatal Çeşme Sk

7

Bab-ı Ali Cad

Şeref Efendi Sk

Nuruosmaniye Cad

Türbedar Sk

Cağaloğlu

Divan Yolu (Ordu) Cad

Sultanahmet

12

Sights

Aya İrini   CHURCH

1 Map p48, C4

Rewbuilt by Justinian in the 540s, the current form of this Byzantine church is almost as old as its near neighbour, Aya Sofya. Used as an arsenal for centuries, it is now open to visitors but the entrance fee is exorbitant considering the fact that there are no exhibits inside. (Hagia Eirene, Church of the Divine Peace; 1st Court, Topkapı Palace; adult/child under 12yr ₺20/free; ☺9am-6pm Wed-Mon mid-Apr–Sep, to 4pm Oct–mid-Apr; 🚊Sultanahmet)

Gülhane Park   PARK

2 Map p48, C2

Gülhane Park was once the outer garden of Topkapı Palace, accessed only by the royal court. These days crowds of locals come here to picnic under the many trees, promenade past the formally planted flowerbeds, and enjoy wonderful views over the Golden Horn and Sea of Marmara from the Set Üstü Çay Bahçesi on the park's northeastern edge. (Gülhane Parkı; 🚊Gülhane)

Carpet Museum   MUSEUM

3 Map p48, D4

Housed in an 18th-century *imaret* (soup kitchen) built behind the Aya Sofya complex, this recently opened museum is entered through a spectacular baroque gate and gives the

Gülhane Park

visitor an excellent overview of the history of Anatolian carpet making. The carpets, which have been sourced from mosques throughout the country, date from the 14th to 20th centuries. (Halı Müzesi; 🕿212-512 6993; www.halimuzesi.com; Soğukçeşme Sokak; admission free; ☺9am-4pm Tue-Sun; 🚊Sultanahmet or Gülhane)

Soğukçeşme Sokak   HISTORIC AREA

4 Map p48, C4

Running between the Topkapı Palace walls and Aya Sofya, this cobbled street is named after the Soğuk Çeşme (Cold Fountain) at its southern end. It is home to the new Carpet Museum, to a row of faux-Ottoman houses functioning as a hotel and to an undoubtedly

Understand

The Ottoman Empire

Rise of a Dynasty

In the 13th century, a Turkish warlord named Osman (b 1258), known as Gazi (Warrior for the Faith), inherited a small territory from his warlord father. Osman's followers became known as Osmanlıs (Ottomans).

Osman died in 1324. His son Orhan captured Bursa from the Byzantines in 1324, made it his base and declared himself sultan of the Ottoman Empire. Thessaloniki was captured from the Venetians in 1387 and Kosovo from the Serbs in 1389, marking the start of the Ottoman expansion into Europe. Soon, the acquisition of the great city of Constantinople and control of the overland trade routes between Europe and Asia became the dynasty's major objective.

In 1451, 21-year-old Mehmet II became sultan. On 29 May 1453, his army breached Constantinople's massive land walls and took control of the city, bringing the Byzantine Empire to an end. Mehmet was given the title Fatih (Conqueror) and began to rebuild and repopulate the city.

Mehmet died in 1481, but the building boom he kicked off was continued by worthy successors including Sultan Selim I (r 1512–20) and Sultan Süleyman I (r 1520–66), known as 'the Magnificent'.

Decline & Fall

After Süleyman's death, the power of the empire slowly disintegrated. In 1683 the Ottoman army was defeated by the Holy Roman Empire at the Battle of Vienna, marking the end of both its military supremacy and the Ottoman expansion into Europe.

A series of incompetent sultans further weakened the empire. There were some exceptions – Selim III (r 1789–1807), who unsuccessfully attempted to modernise the army, and Mahmut II (r 1808–39), who was finally successful in this aim – but they were few and far between. The 19th-century Tanzimat political reforms ushered in by Mahmut II and continued by Abdülmecid I (r 1839–61) took some strides towards modernity, but it was not enough to save the sultanate, which was abolished in 1922. The last of the Osmanlıs to rule as sultan, Mehmet VI (r 1918–22), was expelled from Turkey at this time, and Mustafa Kemal Atatürk became president of the new Turkish Republic.

authentic restored Byzantine cistern that now operates as the hotel restaurant. (🚇Sultanahmet or Gülhane)

Caferağa Medresesi

HISTORIC BUILDING

5 Map p48, C4

This lovely little building tucked away in the shadows of Aya Sofya was designed by Sinan on the orders of Cafer Ağa, Süleyman the Magnificent's chief black eunuch. Built in 1560 as a school, it is now home to a cultural organisation teaching and promoting traditional Turkish handicrafts. The courtyard is home to the pleasant Caferağa Medresesi Çay Bahçesi (p53). (www.tkhv.org; Soğukkuyu Çıkmazı 5, off Caferiye Sokak; admission free; ⏰8.30am-5pm; 🚇Sultanahmet)

Eating

Matbah

OTTOMAN €€€

6 🍴 Map p48, C4

One of a growing number of İstanbul restaurants specialising in so-called 'Ottoman Palace Cuisine', Matbah offers dishes that were first devised in the palace kitchens between the 13th and 19th centuries. The menu changes with the season and features unusual ingredients such as goose. Surrounds are attractive, the staff are attentive and there's live oud music on Friday and Saturday nights. (📞212-514 6151; www.matbahrestaurant.com; Ottoman

Imperial Hotel, Caferiye Sokak 6/1; mezes ₺10-19, mains ₺28-60; ⏰noon-11pm; 📋; 🚇Sultanahmet)

Sefa Restaurant

TURKISH €

7 🍴 Map p48, A4

This popular place near the Grand Bazaar describes its cuisine as Ottoman, but what's really on offer are *hazır yemek* (ready-made dishes) and kebaps at extremely reasonable prices. You can order from an English menu or choose daily specials from the bain marie. Try to arrive early-ish for lunch because many of the dishes run out by 1.30pm. No alcohol. (📞212-520 0670; www.sefarestaurant.com.tr; Nuruosmaniye Caddesi 17, Cağaloğlu; portions ₺8-14, kebaps ₺13-20; ⏰7am-5pm; 📋; 🚇Sultanahmet)

Local Life
Hocapaşa Sokak

If you're in the Sirkeci neighbourhood at lunchtime, join the locals in this pedestrianised street lined with cheap eateries. Here, an array of *lokantas* serve *hazır yemek* (ready-made dishes), **Şehzade Cağ Kebabı** (Map p48, B2; 📞212-520 3361; Hocapaşa Sokak 3a, Sirkeci; kebap ₺15; ⏰11.30am-7.30pm Mon-Sat; 🚇Sirkeci) serves its famous Erzurum-style lamb kebap and the much-loved Hocapaşa Pidecisi offers piping-hot pides accompanied by pickles. For more about eating in Sirkeci, visit www.sirkecirestaurants.com.

Lokum (Turkish delight)

Güvenç Konyalı

TURKISH €

8 Map p48, B2

Specialities from Konya in Central Anatolia are the draw at this bustling place just off the much-loved Hocapaşa Sokak food strip. Regulars come for the spicy *bamya çorbası* (sour soup with lamb and chickpeas), *etli ekmek* (flat bread with meat) and meltingly soft slow-cooked meats from the oven. No alcohol. (☏212-527 5220; Hocapaşa Hamam Sokak 4, Sirkeci; soups ₺8, mains & pides ₺12-25; ⊙7am-9pm Mon-Sat; 🚇Sirkeci)

Hafız Mustafa

SWEETS €

9 Map p48, B2

Making locals happy since 1864, this *şekerleme* (sweets shop) sells *lokum*, baklava, milk puddings, pastries and *börek* (filled pastries). Put your sweet tooth to good use in the upstairs cafe, or choose a selection of indulgences to take home (avoid the baklava, which isn't very good). (www.hafizmustafa. com; Muradiye Caddesi 51, Sirkeci; börek ₺5, baklava ₺6-7.50, puddings ₺6; ⊙7am-2am; 🚇Sirkeci)

Drinking

Set Üstü Çay Bahçesi

TEAHOUSE

10 Map p48, E1

Come to this terraced tea garden to watch the ferries plying the route from Europe to Asia while at the same time enjoying an excellent pot of tea

(1/2 person ₺8/14) accompanied by hot water (such a relief after the usual fiendishly strong Turkish brew). Add a cheap *tost* (toasted cheese sandwich; ₺3) to make a lunch of it. (Gülhane Parkı, Sultanahmet; ⊘9am-10.30pm; ⛎Gülhane)

Caferağa Medresesi Çay Bahçesi   TEA GARDEN

On a fine day, sipping a *çay* in the in the gorgeous courtyard of the Sinan-designed Caferağa Medresesi (see 5 ⊙ Map p48, C4) near Topkapı Palace is a delight. Located close to both Aya Sofya and Topkapı Palace, it's a perfect pitstop between sights. There's simple food available at lunchtime. (Soğukkuyu Çıkmazı 5, off Caferiye Sokak; ⊘8.30am-4pm; ⛎Sultanahmet)

Entertainment

Hocapaşa Culture Centre   PERFORMING ARTS

11 ⭐ Map p48, B2

Occupying a beautifully converted 550-year-old hamam near Eminönü, this cultural centre stages a one-hour whirling dervish performance for tourists on Tuesday, Wednesday, Thursday, Saturday and Sunday evenings at 7pm, and a 1½-hour Turkish dance show on Tuesday, Thursday and Saturday at 9pm. Note that children under seven years are not admitted to the whirling dervish performance. (Hodjapasha Culture Centre; ☎212-511 4626; www.hodjapasha.com; Hocapaşa Hamamı Sokak 3b, Sirkeci; performances adult ₺60-80, child under 12yr ₺40-50; ⛎Sirkeci)

Shopping

Özlem Tuna   JEWELLERY, HOMEWARES

12 🔒 Map p48, B1

A leader in Turkey's contemporary design movement, Özlem Tuna produces super-stylish jewellery and homewares that she sells from her atelier overlooking Sirkeci train station. Her pieces use form and colours that reference the city (tulips, seagulls, gold, Bosphorus blue) and include hamam bowls, coffee and tea sets, serving bowls, trays, rings, earrings, cufflinks and necklaces. (☎212-513 1361; www.ozlemtuna.com; 5th fl, Nemlizade Han, Ankara Caddesi 65, Eminönü; ⊘10am-5pm Mon-Fri, by arrangement Sat; ⛎Sirkeci)

Ali Muhiddin Hacı Bekir   FOOD

13 🔒 Map p48, A1

Many people think that this historic shop, which has been operated by members of the same family for over 200 years, is the best place in the city to buy *lokum*. Choose from *sade* (plain), *cevizli* (walnut), *fıstıklı* (pistachio), *badem* (almond) or *roze* (rose water). There are other branches in Beyoğlu (p97) and Kadıköy. (www.hacibekir.com.tr/eng; Hamidlye Caddesi 31 & 33, Eminönü; ⊘8am-8pm Mon-Sat; ⛎Eminönü)

Explore

Grand Bazaar & the Bazaar District

Crowned by the historic Grand Bazaar (Kapalı Çarşı), this beguiling neighbourhood is also home to the smaller but equally historic Spice Bazaar (Mısır Çarşısı), the upmarket shopping street of Nuruosmaniye Caddesi and the frantically busy shopping precinct around Mahmutpaşa Yokuşu. Presiding over the mercantile mayhem is Süleymaniye Mosque, İstanbul's most magnificent Ottoman mosque.

The Sights in a Day

 The **Grand Bazaar** (p56) is best visited in the morning, when shopkeepers enjoy gossiping with their neighbours over a glass of tea and are less likely to hassle prospective customers. Wander through this ancient shopping mall for two or three hours, stopping for a coffee or tea at one of its cafes before enjoying a kebap lunch at **Gazientep Burç Ocakbaşı** (p67), **Aynen Dürüm** (p68) or **Dürümcü Raif Usta** (p67).

 Visit the **Süleymaniye Mosque** (p60), take a break at **Lale Bahçesi** (p69) or the **Mimar Sinan Teras Cafe** (p70), and then walk down the hill towards the **Spice Bazaar** (p66), popping into the **Rüstem Paşa Mosque** (p63) on the way.

 Siirt Şeref Büryan Kebap (p67) in the Kadınlar Pazarı (Women's Market) in Zeyrek is a great choice for a frills-free dinner. For something more sophisticated, head to **Hamdi Restaurant** (p66), where you can dine on the terrace floor before enjoying a drink and nargile (water pipe) at one of the cafes underneath the Galata Bridge.

For a local's day in the bazaar district, see p62.

Top Sights

Grand Bazaar (p56)

Süleymaniye Mosque (p60)

Local Life

Between the Bazaars (p62)

Best of İstanbul

Shopping

Abdulla Natural Products (p70)

Derviş (p70)

Ümit Berksoy (p70)

Muhlis Günbatlı (p72)

Mekhann (p72)

Yazmacı Necdet Danış (p72)

Altan Şekerleme (p72)

Dhoku (p72)

Ak Gümüş (p73)

Getting There

Walk The Grand Bazaar is a short walk from Sultanahmet.

Tram Alight at Beyazıt-Kapalı Çarşı for the Grand Bazaar, Eminönü for the Spice Bazaar and Laleli-Üniversite for Süleymaniye Mosque.

M Metro The M2 connects Yenikapı with Taksim Meydanı, stopping at Vezneciler near the Grand Bazaar and Süleymaniye Mosque; and also on the new bridge across the Golden Horn.

Top Sights
Grand Bazaar

When Mehmet the Conqueror laid the Kapalı Çarşı's foundation stone in 1455, he gave the imperial imprimatur to a local mercantile tradition that has remained strong ever since. Located in the centre of the Old City, this atmospheric covered market is the heart of İstanbul in much more than a geographic sense – artisans learn their trade here, businessmen negotiate important deals and tourists make a valuable contribution to the local economy (sometimes, it must be said, against their better judgements).

Kapalı Çarşı, Covered Market

◉ Map p18, G4

🕑 8.30am-7pm Mon-Sat

Ⓜ Vezneciler, 🚋 Beyazıt-Kapalı Çarşı

Don't Miss

Nuruosmaniye Mosque & Gate

Built in Ottoman baroque style between 1748 and 1755, this mosque is located on the busy pedestrian route from Cağaloğlu Meydanı and Nuruosmaniye Caddesi to the bazaar, but is surprisingly peaceful inside. It is located next to one of the major entrances to the Grand Bazaar, the Nuruosmaniye Kapısı (Nuruosmaniye Gate, Gate 1), which is adorned with a golden *tuğra* (crest of the sultan).

Kalpakçılar Caddesi

Shop windows crammed with glittering gold jewellery line both sides of the bazaar's busiest thoroughfare. Originally named after the makers of *kalpakçılars* (fur hats) who had their stores here, it's now full of jewellers who pay up to US$90,000 per year in rent for this high-profile location. In recent years chain retail stores have begun to open outlets along its length, triggering protests by the bazaar's traditional artisans.

Sandal Bedesteni

A majestic space featuring 20 small domes, this 16th-century stone warehouse was built during the reign of Süleyman the Magnificent and has always been used for the storage and sale of fabric. Unfortunately, the current wares don't include the fine *sandal* (fabric woven with silk) that was sold here in the past.

İç (Inner) Bedesten

Also known as the Eski (Old) Bedesten, this is the oldest part of the bazaar and has always been an area where precious items are stored and sold. These days it's where most of the bazaar's antique stores are located. Also here are top-quality jewellers such as Ümit Berksoy (p70).

☑ **Top Tips**

▶ To visit ateliers where traditional artisans work, sign up for the Grand Bazaar Walk (not the Shopping Tour) conducted by İstanbul Walks (www.istanbul-walks.com).

▶ There are photographic opportunities galore in the bazaar; İstanbulodos (www.istanbulodosviaggio.com) runs specialist photographic tours.

▶ Bargaining is an accepted practice in traditional carpet, antique and jewellery shops, but the chic homewares shops have fixed prices.

✕ **Take a Break**

Cafes are scattered throughout the bazaar. Our favourites include Şark Kahvesi (p69) and Ethem Tezçakar Kahveci (p69).

For a cheap and tasty lunch, head to Bahar Restaurant (p68), close to the Nuruosmaniye Gate; Aynen Dürüm (p68), just inside the Kılıççılar Gate; or Gaziantep Burç Ocakbaşı (p67) off Yağlıkçılar Caddesi.

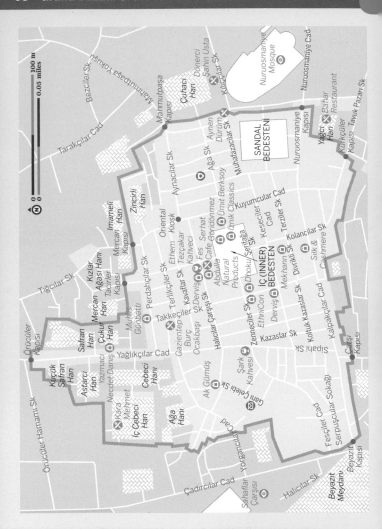

Halıcılar Çarşışı Sokak

The most photogenic street in the bazaar is also the most enticing. Home to designer stores such as Abdulla Natural Products (p70) and Derviş (p70), it also has a number of popular cafes.

Kuyumcular Caddesi

The name of this street pays tribute to the *kuyumcular* (jewellers) who have always been based here; these days it's the centre of the bazaar's silver merchants. Also here is one of the bazaar's most unusual features, a quaint 19th-century timber structure known as the **Oriental Kiosk**. Once home to the most famous *muhallebici* (milk pudding shop) in the district, it now functions as a jewellery store.

Zincirli Han

Accessed off Kuyumcular Caddesi and named after the *zincirli* (chains) that were once manufactured here, this pretty cobbled caravanserai is now home to one of the bazaar's best-known carpet merchants.

Takkeçiler Sokak

This charming street is known for its marble *sebils* (public drinking fountains) and shops selling kilims (pileless woven rugs). These include designer stores such as Dhoku (p72)

and EthniCon, which offer kilims featuring modern and avant-garde designs.

Textile Stores

Many of the best textile stores in İstanbul are located on or near the bazaar's major north–south axis – Sipahi Sokak and Yağlıkçılar Caddesi. The crush of shoppers here can occasionally resemble a cavalry charge (in Turkish, *sipahi* means 'cavalry soldier'), but it's worth braving the crowds to visit famous stores such as Yazmacı Necdet Danış (p72), which sells a wonderful array of fabrics.

İç Cebeci Han

This is one of the largest of the bazaar's many caravanserais. In Ottoman times it would have offered travelling merchants accommodation and a place to do business; these days it's home to artisans' workshops, a branch of the Derviş bathwares shop and a popular *kebapçı* (kebap eatery) called Kara Mehmet.

Sahaflar Çarşısı

The 'Secondhand Book Bazaar' has operated as a book and paper market since Byzantine times. At the centre of its shady courtyard is a bust of İbrahim Müteferrika (1674–1745), who printed the first book in Turkey in 1732.

Top Sights
Süleymaniye Mosque

Commissioned by Süleyman the Magnificent in 1550, the Süleymaniye was the fourth imperial mosque built in İstanbul and it certainly lives up to its patron's nickname. Crowning one of İstanbul's seven hills, it's the Old City's major landmark and the spiritual hub of the Bazaar District. Though not the largest of the city's Ottoman-era mosques, it is unusual in that many of its original *külliye* (mosque complex) buildings have been retained and sympathetically adapted for re-use.

⊙ Map p18, E2

Professor Sıddık Sami Onar Caddesi

ⓂVezneciler, **Ⓖ**Laleli-Üniversite

Don't Miss

Minarets

The four minarets with their 10 beautiful *şerefes* (balconies) are said to represent the fact that Süleyman was the fourth of the Ottoman sultans to rule the city and the 10th sultan after the establishment of the empire.

Interior

The mosque's architect, Mimar Sinan, incorporated four buttresses into the walls of the building – the result is open, airy and highly reminiscent of Aya Sofya, especially as the dome is nearly as large as the one crowning the great Byzantine basilica. Also notable is the *mihrab* (prayer niche indicating the direction of Mecca), which is decorated with fine İznik tiles.

Tombs

To the right (southeast) of the main entrance is the cemetery, home to the *türbes* (tombs) of Süleyman and his wife Haseki Hürrem Sultan (Roxelana). The tilework in both is superb, as is the stained glass in Roxelana's tomb.

İmaret

The mosque's *imaret* (soup kitchen) is on its northwestern edge and its tranquil courtyard is a lovely place to enjoy a çay.

Tiryaki Çarşısı

The street facing the mosque's main entrance is now called Professor Sıddık Sami Onar Caddesi, but was formerly known as the Tiryaki Çarşısı (Market of the Addicts) as it was home to teahouses selling opium. These now house popular *fasulye* (bean) restaurants including Kuru Fasulyeci Erzincanlı Ali Baba (p68).

☑ Top Tips

▶ In the garden behind the mosque is a terrace with lovely views of the Golden Horn (Haliç).

▶ The surrounding streets are home to many Ottoman timber houses. To see some, head down Fetva Yokuşu and then veer right into Namahrem Sokak and into Ayrancı Sokak.

▶ Visitors to the mosque must remove their shoes; women should cover their heads with a scarf or shawl.

▶ Avoid visiting at lunchtime on Friday, when weekly sermons and group prayers are held.

✕ Take a Break

For an unusual pick-me-up, head down the streets southwest of the mosque to sample *boza* at historic Vefa Bozacısı (p70).

The panoramic terrace of the Mimar Sinan Teras Cafe (p70), located in the street beneath the mosque, is a great choice for a tea and nargile break.

Local Life
Between the Bazaars

Locals outnumber tourists by a generous margin in the crowded and cacophanous streets surrounding the Grand and Spice Bazaars. Here, housewives source bargains, street vendors hawk fresh fruit and pastries, and the atmosphere crackles with good-humoured energy.

1 **Mahmutpaşa Kapısı**
Exit the Grand Bazaar by this gate (gate 18) and you'll find yourself on the busy thoroughfare of Mahmutpaşa Yokuşu, which runs down to the Spice Bazaar and is home to shops selling everything from coffee cups to circumcision outfits

2 **Delicious Döner Kebaps**
Ask any shopkeeper in the Grand Bazaar about who makes the best döner kebap (spit-roasted lamb slices) in the immediate area, and

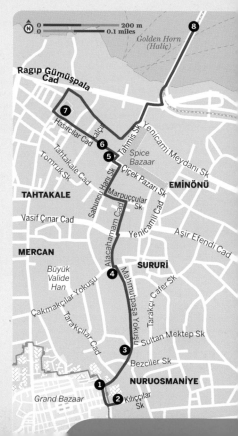

they are likely to give the same answer: 'Şahin Usta, of course!' Grab one to go from **Dönerci Şahin Usta** (☎212-526 5297; www.donercisahinusta.com; Kılıççılar Sokak 7-9, Nuruosmaniye; döner kebap from ₺7; ☺11am-3pm Mon-Sat; 🚇Çemberlitaş).

❸ Mahmutpaşa Hamamı

One of the oldest Ottoman hamams in the city (it dates from 1476), this building was converted into a down-market shopping centre a decade or so ago. Its domed ceiling, stained-glass windows and marble floor offer a glimpse of its former glory.

❹ Islamic Chic

In Bebek and Beyoğlu the fashion might be for tight jeans, revealing jackets and chunky jewellery, but here in the Old City there's little make-up and even less flesh on show. Wildly popular **Armine** (www.armine.com; Mahmutpaşa Yokuşu 181, Eminönü; ☺10am-6pm Mon-Sat; 🚇Eminönü) is where Zara style meets the headscarf.

❺ Turkish Coffee to Take Home

Tahmis Sokak on the western edge of the Spice Bazaar hosts a jumble of stalls selling slabs of pungent farmhouse cheese, tubs of olives and mounds of *biber salçası* (hot pepper paste). Also here is the flagship store of Turkey's most famous coffee purveyor, **Kurukahveci Mehmet Efendi** (www.mehmetefendi.com/eng; cnr Tahmis Sokak & Hasırcılar Caddesi, Eminönü; ☺9am-6pm Mon-Sat; 🚇Eminönü).

❻ Hasırcılar Caddesi

The shops lining this narrow street running parallel to the Golden Horn sell everything from teapots to toothbrushes. Stock up on provisions or pop into **Develi Baklava** (☎212-512 1261; Hasırcılar Caddesi 89, Eminönü; portion ₺8-9; ☺6.30am-7pm Mon-Sat; 🚇Haliç, 🚇Eminönü) to sample what may well be İstanbul's most delicious sweet treat.

❼ Rüstem Paşa Mosque

This diminutive mosque is a gem. Dating from 1560, it was designed by Mimar Sinan for Rüstem Paşa, son-in-law and grand vizier of Süleyman the Magnificent. A showpiece of the best Ottoman architecture and tilework, it's accessed via stairs off Hasırcılar Caddesi or off a side street to the right (north). Avoid visiting during prayer times, when local shopkeepers worship here.

❽ Galata Bridge

This İstanbul icon carries a constant flow of locals crossing between Beyoğlu and Eminönü, hopeful anglers trailing their lines into the waters below, and a constantly changing procession of street vendors hawking everything from fresh-baked *simits* (sesame-encrusted bread rings) to Rolex rip-offs. Consider enjoying a beer and nargile while watching the ferries ply the surrounding waters.

Sights

Spice Bazaar
MARKET

1 ◎ Map p64, H1

Vividly coloured spices are displayed alongside jewel-like *lokum* (Turkish delight) at this Ottoman-era marketplace, providing eye candy for the thousands of tourists and locals who make their way here every day. As well as spices, stalls sell caviar, dried herbs, nuts and dried fruits. The number of stalls selling tourist trinkets increases annually, yet this remains a great place to stock up on edible souvenirs, share a few jokes with the vendors and marvel at the well-preserved building.

Local Life
Kadınlar Pazarı (Women's Market)

Hidden behind the majestic Aqueduct of Valens in Fatih, this fascinating market (Map p64, A2) is full of restaurants and shops specialising in freshly slaughtered meat, so it's not for the faint-hearted. Lamb carcasses hang outside butcher shops and tubs of smelly dried sheep's heads are common. Less confrontational are the bins of aromatic spices, colourful strings of dried chillies and street carts selling fresh fruit and vegetables. After exploring, be sure to enjoy a meal at one of the eateries specialising in tasty meat dishes from the southeastern city of Siirt.

(Mısır Çarşısı, Egyptian Market; ◎8am-6pm Mon-Sat, 8am-7pm Sun; 🚈Eminönü)

New Mosque
MOSQUE

2 ◎ Map p64, H1

Only in İstanbul would a 400-year-old mosque be called 'New'. Dating from 1597, its design references both the Blue Mosque and the Süleymaniye Mosque, with a large forecourt and a square sanctuary surmounted by a series of semidomes crowned by a grand dome. The interior is richly decorated with gold leaf, coloured İznik tiles and carved marble. (Yeni Camii; Yenicamii Meydanı Sokak, Eminönü; 🚈Eminönü)

Eating

Fatih Damak Pide
PIDE €

3 🍴 Map p64, A2

It's worth making the trek to this *pideci* (pizza place) overlooking the Fatih İtfaiye Park near the Aqueduct of Valens, as its reputation for making the best Karadeniz (Black Sea)–style pide (Turkish-style pizza) on the Historic Peninsula is well deserved and the free pots of tea served with meals are a nice touch. (📞212-521 5057; www.fatihdamak-pide.com; Büyük Karaman Caddesi 48, Zeyrek; pide ₺12-16; ◎11am-11pm; Ⓜ Vezneciler)

Hamdi Restaurant
KEBAP €€

4 🍴 Map p64, G1

Hamdi Arpacı arrived in İstanbul in the 1960s and almost immediately established a street stand near the Spice Bazaar where he grilled and sold tasty kebaps made according to recipes from his hometown Urfa, in Turkey's southeast. His kebaps became so popular with locals that he soon acquired this nearby building, which has phenomenal views from its top-floor terrace. (📞212-528 8011; www.hamdirestorant.com.tr; Kalçın Sokak 17, Eminönü; mezes ₺9-14, kebaps ₺25-32; Ⓜ Haliç, 🚋 Eminönü)

Siirt Şeref Büryan Kebap
ANATOLIAN €

5 🍴 Map p64, A2

Those who enjoy investigating regional cuisines should head to this four-storey eatery in the Kadınlar Pazarı (Women's Market) near the Aqueduct of Valens. It specialises in two dishes that are a speciality of the southeastern city of Siirt: *büryan* (lamb slow-cooked in a pit) and *perde pilavi* (chicken and rice cooked in pastry). Both are totally delicious. (📞212-635 8085; www.serefburyan. com; İtfaye Caddesi 4, Kadınlar Pazarı; büryan ₺12, perde pilavi ₺12; ⏱9.30am-10pm Sep-May, till midnight Jun-Aug; Ⓜ Vezneciler)

Gazientep Burç Ocakbaşı
KEBAP €

6 🍴 Map p64, F4

The *üsta* (master chef) at this simple place presides over a charcoal grill where choice cuts of meat are cooked to perfection. You can claim a stool or ask for a *dürüm* kebap (meat wrapped in bread) to go. We particularly

Spice Bazaar

recommend the spicy Adana kebap and the delectable dolması (eggplant and red peppers stuffed with rice and herbs). (Parçacılar Sokak 12, off Yağlıkçılar Caddesi, Grand Bazaar; kebaps ₺13-22; ⏱noon-4pm Mon-Sat; Ⓜ Vezneciler, 🚋 Beyazıt-Kapalı Çarşı)

Dürümcü Raif Usta
KEBAP €

7 🍴 Map p64, H4

The assembly line of staff assisting the *üsta* at this place attests to the excellence and popularity of its Adana or Urfa *dürüm* kebap. Note that the Adana is spicy, Urfa isn't. (📞212-528 5997; Küçük Yıldız Han Sokak 6, Mahmutpaşa; dürüm kebap ₺9; ⏱11.30am-6pm Mon-Sat; 🚋 Çemberlitaş)

◯ Local Life
Fish Sandwiches

The city's favourite fast-food treat is undoubtedly the *balık ekmek* (fish sandwich), and the most atmospheric place to try one is at the Eminönü end of the Galata Bridge (Map p64, H1). Here, in front of fishing boats tied to the quay, are a number of stands where mackerel fillets are grilled, crammed into fresh bread and served with salad; a generous squeeze of bottled lemon is optional but recommended. A sandwich will set you back a mere ₺6 or so, and is delicious accompanied by a glass of the *şalgam* (sour turnip juice) sold by nearby pickle vendors.

Aynen Dürüm
KEBAP ₺

8 Map p64, G4

Just inside the Grand Bazaar's Kılıççılar Kapısı (Kılıççılar Gate), near where the currency dealers ply their noisy trade, is this perennially busy place. Patrons are free to doctor their choice of meat (we like the chicken) with pickled cucumber, grilled and picked green chillies, parsley, sumac and other accompaniments that are laid out on the communal bench. (Muhafazacılar Sokak 29; dürüm kebap ₺8; ⊙7am-6pm Mon-Sat; 🚇Çemberlitaş)

Bahar Restaurant
TURKISH ₺

9 Map p64, G5

Tiny Bahar ('Spring') is popular with local shopkeepers and is always full, so arrive early to score a table. Dishes change daily and with the season – try the flavourful lentil soup, tasty *hünkar beğendi* (literally 'Sultan's Delight'; lamb or beef stew served on a mound of rich eggplant puree) or creamy macaroni. The latter is made only once per week. No alcohol. (Yağcı Han 13, off Nuruosmaniye Sokak, Nuruosmaniye; soup ₺5, dishes ₺10-17; ⊙11am-4pm Mon-Sat; 🚇Çemberlitaş)

Fes Cafe
CAFE ₺₺

10 Map p64, H5

After a morning spent trading repartee with the touts in the Grand Bazaar, you'll be in need of a respite. Those who want a cafe with a Western-style ambiance and menu are sure to be happy with this stylish cafe just outside the Nuruosmaniye Gate. Sandwiches, salads and pastas feature on the menu. There's a second branch inside the Grand Bazaar. (Ali Baba Türbe Sokak 25, Nuruosmaniye; sandwiches ₺14-22, salads ₺16-20; pasta ₺18-20; ⊙closed Sun; 📶; 🚇Çemberlitaş)

Kuru Fasulyeci Erzincanlı Ali Baba
TURKISH ₺

11 Map p64, D2

Join the crowds of hungry locals at this long-time favourite opposite the Süleymaniye Mosque. It's been dishing up its signature *kuru fasulye* (white beans cooked in a spicy tomato sauce) accompanied by pilaf (rice) and pickles since 1924. The next-door *fasulyeci* (restaurant specialising in beans) is nearly as old and serves up more of the same. No alcohol. (www.kurufasulyeci.com; Professor Sıddık Sami Onar Caddesi 11, Süleymaniye; beans with pilaf & pickles ₺12; ⏰7am-7pm; ⏹; Ⓜ Vezneciler, 🚋 Laleli-Üniversite)

Drinking

Erenler Nargile ve Çay Bahçesi
TEA GARDEN

12 Map p64, F5

Set in the vine-covered courtyard of the Çorlulu Ali Paşa Medrese, this nargile cafe near the Grand Bazaar is the most atmospheric in the Old City. (Yeniçeriler Caddesi 35, Beyazıt; ⏰7am-midnight, 🚋 Beyazıt-Kapalı Çarşı)

Lale Bahçesi
TEA GARDEN

13 Map p64, D2

Make your way down the stairs into the sunken courtyard opposite the Süleymaniye Mosque to discover this charming outdoor teahouse,

which is popular with students from the nearby theological college and İstanbul University. (Şifahane Caddesi, Süleymaniye; ⏰9am-11pm; Ⓜ Vezneciler, 🚋 Laleli-Üniversite)

Ethem Tezçakar Kahveci
CAFE

14 Map p64, G4

Bekir Tezçakar's family has been at the helm of this tiny coffee shop for four generations. Smack bang in the middle of the bazaar's most glamorous retail strip, its traditional brass-tray tables and wooden stools are a good spot to enjoy a break and watch the passing parade of shoppers. (Halıcılar Çarşışı Sokak, Grand Bazaar; ⏰8.30am-7pm Mon-Sat; Ⓜ Vezneciler, 🚋 Beyazıt-Kapalı Çarşı)

Şark Kahvesi
CAFE

15 Map p64, F5

The Şark's arched ceiling betrays its former existence as part of a bazaar street; years ago some enterprising *kahveci* (coffeehouse owner) walled up several sides and turned it into a

---

Understand
Ottoman Hans

Built by rich merchants, *hans* (caravanserais) enabled caravans to unload and trade their spices, furs, silks and slaves right in the thick of the bazaar action. Typically two- to three-storey arcaded buildings set around a courtyard where animals could be housed, they differed from Persian-style caravanserais in that they were used as storage and trading spaces as well as for short-term accommodation. Although *hans* are found all over Turkey, the concentration in İstanbul is unrivalled, a testament to the city's importance as a trading-route hub. Sadly, most are in a dilapidated state today.

Local Life

Mimar Sinan Teras Cafe

A magnificent panorama of the city can be enjoyed from the spacious outdoor terrace of this popular student **cafe** (Map p64 E1; ☎212-514 4414; www.mimarsinanterascafe.com; Mimar Sinan Han, Fetva Yokuşu 34-35, Süleymaniye; ⊗8am-1am; MVezneciler or Haliç, ⬛Laleli-Üniversite) in a ramshackle building located in the shadow of the Süleymaniye Mosque. Come here during the day or in the evening to admire the view over a coffee, unwind with a nargile or enjoy a glass of çay and game of backgammon.

cafe. Located on one of the bazaar's major thoroughfares, it's popular with both stallholders and tourists. (Oriental Coffeeshop; Yağlıkçılar Caddesi 134, Grand Bazaar; ⊗8.30am-7pm Mon-Sat; MVezneciler, ⬛Beyazıt-Kapalı Çarşı)

Vefa Bozacısı
BOZA BAR

 Map p64, B2

This famous *boza* bar was established in 1876 and locals still flock here to drink the viscous tonic, which is made from water, sugar and fermented barley and has a slight lemony tang. Topped with dried chickpeas and a sprinkle of cinnamon, it has a reputation for building up strength and virility, and tends to be an acquired taste. (www.vefa.com.tr; cnr Vefa & Katip Çelebi Caddesis, Molla Hüsrev; boza ₺3; ⊗8am-midnight; MVezneciler, ⬛Laleli-Üniversite)

Shopping

Abdulla Natural Products
TEXTILES, BATHWARE

 Map p64, G4

The first of the Western-style designer stores to appear in this ancient marketplace, Abdulla sells top-quality cotton bed linen and towels, handspun woollen throws from eastern Turkey, cotton *peştemals* (bath wraps) and pure olive-oil soap. There's another branch in the Fes Cafe (p68). (www.abdulla.com; Halıcılar Çarşışı Sokak 62, Grand Bazaar; ⊗8.30am-7pm Mon-Sat; MVezneciler, ⬛Beyazıt-Kapalı Çarşı)

Derviş
TEXTILES, BATHWARE

 Map p64, F5

Gorgeous raw cotton and silk *peştemals* share shelf space here with traditional Turkish dowry vests and engagement dresses. If these don't take your fancy, the pure olive-oil soaps and old hamam bowls are sure to step into the breach. There are other branches in Halıcılar Çarşışı Sokak and in the Cebeci Han, also in the bazaar. (www.dervis.com; Keseciler Caddesi 33-35, Grand Bazaar; ⊗8.30am-7pm Mon-Sat; MVezneciler, ⬛Beyazıt-Kapalı Çarşı)

Ümit Berksoy
JEWELLERY

 Map p64, G4

Jeweller Ümit Berksoy handcrafts gorgeous Byzantine-style rings, earrings and necklaces using gold and old coins as well as more contemporary pieces

Understand

İstanbul in Print

This colourful and complex city has inspired writers throughout history, and continues to do so today. Local luminaries including Orhan Pamuk and Elif Şafak set most of their novels here, and many foreign writers have used the city as a literary setting.

Local Writers

İrfan Orga's 1950 masterpiece *Portrait of a Turkish Family* is among the best writing about the city ever published, as is *A Mind at Peace* (1949) by Ahmet Hamdi Tanıpar. Elif Şafak's *The Flea Palace* (2002) and *The Bastard of Istanbul* (2006) and Izzet Celasin's *Black Sky, Black Sea* (2012) are more recent novels set in İstanbul.

Nobel laureate Orhan Pamuk has set most of his novels here, including *Cevdet Bey & His Sons* (1982), *The White Castle* (1985), *The Black Book* (1990), *The New Life* (1995), *My Name is Red* (1998) and *The Museum of Innocence* (2009). In 2005 he published a memoir, *Istanbul: Memories of a City*.

Literary Visitors

Foreign novelists and travel writers have long tried to capture the magic and mystery of İstanbul in their work. One of the earliest to do so was French novelist Pierre Loti, whose novel *Aziyadé* (1879) introduced Europe to Loti's almond-eyed Turkish lover and to the mysterious and all-pervasive attractions of the city itself. Another notable work from this period is *Constantinople* (1878) by Italian writer Edmondo De Amicis.

Historical novels set here include *The Rage of the Vulture* (Barry Unsworth; 1982), *The Stone Woman* (Tariq Ali; 2001), *The Calligrapher's Night* (Yasmine Ghata; 2006) and *The Dark Angel* (Mika Waltari; 1952).

The city also features as the setting for some great crime novels and thrillers, including Barbara Nadel's Inspector İkmen novels; Joseph Kanon's *Istanbul Passage* (2012); Jason Goodwin's Yashim the Ottoman Investigator novels; Jenny White's Kamil Paşa novels; Mehmet Murat Somer's Hop-Çıkı-Yaya series of gay crime novels; Esmahan Aykol's Kati Hirschel Murder Mysteries; and Eric Ambler's *The Mask of Dimitrios* (1939), *Journey into Fear* (1940) and *The Light of Day* (1962).

at his tiny atelier just outside the İç Bedesten. (☏212-522 3391; İnciler Sokak 2-6, Grand Bazaar; ⏱8.30am-7pm Mon-Sat; Ⓜ Vezneciler, 🚋Beyazıt-Kapalı Çarşı)

Muhlis Günbattı   TEXTILES

20 🔒 Map p64, F4

One of the most famous stores in the Grand Bazaar, Muhlis Günbattı specialises in *suzani* (needlework) fabrics from Uzbekistan. These beautiful bedspreads, tablecloths and wall hangings are made from fine cotton embroidered with silk. As well as the textiles, it stocks top-quality carpets, brightly coloured kilims and a small range of antique Ottoman fabrics richly embroidered with gold. (www. muhlisgunbatti.net; Perdahçılar Sokak 48, Grand Bazaar; ⏱8.30am-7pm Mon-Sat; Ⓜ Vezneciler, 🚋Beyazıt-Kapalı Çarşı)

Mekhann   TEXTILES

21 🔒 Map p64, G5

Bolts of richly coloured hand-woven silk from Uzbekistan and a range of finely woven shawls join finely embroidered bedspreads and pillow slips on the crowded shelves of this Grand Bazaar store, which sets the bar high when it comes to quality. (☏212-519 9444; Divrikli Sokak 49, Grand Bazaar; ⏱8.30am-7pm Mon-Sat; Ⓜ Vezneciler, 🚋Beyazıt-Kapalı Çarşı)

Yazmacı Necdet Danış   TEXTILES

22 🔒 Map p64, F4

Fashion designers and buyers from every corner of the globe know that when in İstanbul, this is where to come to source top-quality textiles. It's crammed with bolts of fabric of every description – shiny, simple, sheer and sophisticated – as well as *peştemals,* scarves and clothes. Murat Danış next door is part of the same operation. (Yağlıkçılar Caddesi 57, Grand Bazaar; ⏱8.30am-7pm Mon-Sat; Ⓜ Vezneciler, 🚋Beyazıt-Kapalı Çarşı)

Altan Şekerleme   FOOD & DRINK

23 🔒 Map p64, E1

It's not just kids who like candy stores. İstanbullus of every age have been coming to this shop in the Küçük Pazar (Little Bazaar) precinct below the Süleymaniye Mosque since 1865, lured by its cheap and delectable *lokum, helva* (sweet made from sesame seeds) and *akide* (hard candy). (☏212-522 5909; www.altansekerleme.com; Kible Çeşme Caddesi 68, Eminönü; ⏱8am-7pm Mon-Sat, 9am-6pm Sun; Ⓜ Haliç, 🚋Eminönü)

Dhoku   CARPETS

24 🔒 Map p64, G5

One of the new generation of rug stores opening in the bazaar, Dhoku (meaning 'texture') sells artfully designed wool kilims in resolutely modernist designs. Its sister store, **EthniCon** (www.ethnicon.com; Takkeçiler Sokak, Grand Bazaar), opposite this store, sells similarly stylish rugs in vivid colours and can be said to have started the current craze in contemporary kilims. (www.dhoku.com; Takkeçiler Sokak 58-60, Grand Bazaar; ⏱8.30am-7pm Mon-Sat; Ⓜ Vezneciler, 🚋Beyazıt-Kapalı Çarşı)

Jewellery for sale in the Grand Bazaar (p56)

Ak Gümüş   HANDICRAFTS

25 🏠 Map p64, F4

Specialising in Central Asian tribal arts, this delightful store stocks an array of felt toys and hats, as well as jewellery and other objects made using coins and beads. (Gani Çelebi Sokak 8, Grand Bazaar; ⊘9am-7pm Mon-Sat; 🚊Beyazıt-Kapalı Çarşı, 🚊Vezneciler)

Sofa   ART, JEWELLERY

26 🏠 Map p64, H5

Investigation of Sofa's three floors of artfully arranged clutter reveals an eclectic range of pricey jewellery, prints, textiles, calligraphy, Ottoman miniatures and contemporary Turkish art. (☎212-520 2850; www.kashifsofa.com; Nuruosmaniye Caddesi 53, Nuruosmaniye; ⊘9.30am-6.30pm Mon-Sat; 🚊Çemberlitaş)

Silk & Cashmere   CLOTHING

27 🏠 Map p64, H5

The Nuruosmaniye branch of this popular chain sells cashmere and silk-cashmere-blend cardigans, jumpers, tops and shawls. All are remarkably well priced considering their quality. There's another, smaller, store inside the Grand Bazaar. (www.silkcashmere. com; Nuruosmaniye Caddesi 69, Nuruosmaniye; ⊘9.30am-7pm Mon-Sat; 🚊Çemberlitaş)

Top Sights
Kariye Museum (Chora Church)

Getting There

The Kariye Museum is 5km west of Sultanahmet.

🚌 Lines 31E, 32, 36K and 38E from Eminönü, 87 from Taksim; Edirnekapı stop.

⚓ Golden Horn (Haliç) line; Ayvansaray stop.

İstanbul has more than its fair share of Byzantine monuments, but few are as drop-dead gorgeous as this mosaic-laden church. Nestled in the shadow of Theodosius II's monumental land walls and now a museum overseen by the Aya Sofya curators, it receives a fraction of the visitor numbers that its big sister attracts but offers an equally fascinating insight into Byzantine art. Virtually all of the interior decoration – the famous mosaics and the less renowned but equally striking frescoes – dates from 1312.

Mosaic of Mary and the Baby Jesus

Don't Miss

Inner Narthex

Highlights in the second of the inner corridors include the *Khalke Jesus,* which shows Christ and Mary with two donors. The southern dome features a stunning depiction of Jesus and his ancestors (the *Genealogy of Christ*) and the northern dome features a serenely beautiful mosaic of Mary and the Baby Jesus surrounded by her ancestors.

Nave

In the nave are mosaics of Christ; of Mary and the Baby Jesus; and of the *Assumption of the Blessed Virgin* – turn around to see this, as it's over the main door you just entered. The 'infant' being held by Jesus is actually Mary's soul.

Parecclesion

This side chapel was built to hold the tombs of the church's founder and relatives. It's decorated with frescoes depicting scenes taken from the Old Testament; most deal with the themes of death and resurrection. The striking painting in the apse shows a powerful Christ raising Adam and Eve out of their sarcophagi, with saints and kings in attendance.

The Chora's Patron

Most of the interior decoration was funded by Theodore Metochites, a poet and man of letters who was auditor of the treasury under Emperor Andronikos II (r 1282–1328). One of the museum's most wonderful mosaics, found above the door to the nave in the inner narthex, depicts Theodore offering the church to Christ.

Kariye Müzesi

http://ayasofyamuzesi.gov.tr

Kariye Camii Sokak, Edirnekapı

admission ₺15

🕙9am-6pm Thu-Tue mid-Apr–Sep, to 5pm Oct–mid-Apr

☑ Top Tips

▶ The best way to visit Edirnekapı is to take the Golden Horn (Haliç) ferry, alight at Ayvansaray and walk up the hill alongside the historic city walls.

▶ The museum is currently undergoing a major restoration. Before visiting, check that the parecclesion and outer and inner narthexes are open.

✕ Take a Break

Dishes devised for the palace kitchens at Topkapı, Edirne and Dolmabahçe are on offer at **Asitane** (www.asitanerestaurant.com; Kariye Oteli, Kariye Camii Sokak 6; mains ₺32-50; 🕙11am-midnight; 🖉) in the next-door Kariye Hotel.

Explore

İstiklal Caddesi & Beyoğlu

This is the city's high-octane hub of eating, drinking and entertainment, full of crowded restaurants, glamorous rooftop bars and live-music venues. Built around the pedestrianised boulevard of İstiklal Caddesi, it incorporates bohemian residential districts such as Çukurcuma and Cihangir, bustling entertainment enclaves such as Asmalımescit, the historically rich pocket of Galata and the hipster haven of Karaköy.

The Sights in a Day

☀ Begin your day at **Taksim Meydanı** (Taksim Sq; p79), the symbolic heart of both Beyoğlu and the modern city. From here, wander down **İstiklal Caddesi** (p78), being sure to visit the Balık Pazarı, SALT Beyoğlu and ARTER. Stop for coffee at **Manda Batmaz** (p90), then visit Orhan Pamuk's **Museum of Innocence** (p87) and the surrounding district of Çukurcuma, home to many of the city's antique shops.

☼ Dedicate your afternoon to art. Begin at the **İstanbul Modern** (p80), viewing its diverse collection of Turkish and international art, then saunter through neighbouring Karaköy, enjoying a coffee or tea at **Karabatak** (p92) or **Dem** (p92), lunch at **Lokanta Maya** (p90) or the delicious baklava at **Karaköy Güllüoğlu** (p88).

☾ Beyoğlu is known for its rooftop bars, so start your evening at **Mikla** (p91), **360** (p91) or **NuTeras** (p93). Then move on to a traditional eatery to eat, drink and make merry *à la Turka* – **Çukur Meyhane** (p90), **Klemuri** (p88) and **Zübeyir Ocakbaşı** (p88) are all great options. Kick on to a club, or wind down at the **Tophane Nargile Cafes** (p93).

For a local's day in Beyoğlu, see p82.

Top Sights

Q Local Life

♥ Best of İstanbul

Getting There

🚋 **Tram** The tram from Sultanahmet stops at Eminönü, crosses Galata Bridge and then stops at Karaköy, Tophane, Fındıklı and Kabataş.

Funicular Funiculars link Karaköy with Tünel Meydanı and Kabataş with Taksim Meydanı.

Ⓜ **Metro** The M2 connects Yenikapı with Taksim Meydanı, stopping at a station on the new bridge across the Golden Horn (Haliç) and at Şişhane near Tünel Meydanı.

Top Sights
İstiklal Caddesi

Once called the Grand Rue de Pera but renamed İstiklal (Independence) in the early years of the Republic, Beyoğlu's premier boulevard is a perfect metaphor for 21st-century Turkey. A long pedestrianised strip full of shops, cafes, cinemas and cultural centres, it showcases İstanbul's Janus-like personality, embracing modernity one minute and happily bowing to tradition the next. Come here to experience the city as the locals do, promenading the street's length and taking advantage of its many eating, drinking and shopping opportunities.

Independence Ave

◉ Map p84, C2

Don't Miss

Taksim Meydanı

Named after the 18th-century stone *taksim* (water storage unit) on its western side, this square is home to an architecturally significant cultural centre and an often-overlooked monument to the founding of the Republic. In recent years, it has also been the site of major anti-government demonstrations.

Çiçek Pasajı

Built in 1876 and decorated in Second Empire style, the Cité de Pera building once housed a shopping arcade and apartments. The arcade is now known as the Çiçek Pasajı (Flower Passage) and is full of boisterous *meyhanes* (taverns).

Balık Pazarı

Next to the Çiçek Pasajı, Galatasaray's fish market is full of small stands selling *midye tava* (skewered mussels fried in hot oil), *kokoreç* (skewered lamb or mutton intestines seasoned and grilled over charcoal) and fresh produce.

SALT Beyoğlu

Occupying a former apartment building dating from the 1850s, this three-level **cultural centre** (☑212-377 4200; www.saltonline.org/en; İstiklal Caddesi 136; ⏱noon-8pm Tue-Sat, to 6pm Sun; Ⓜ Şişhane, 🚇 Karaköy, then funicular to Tünel) offers exhibition spaces, a walk-in cinema and a bookshop.

ARTER

This four-floor **contemporary arts space** (☑212-243 3767; www.arter.org.tr; İstiklal Caddesi 211; admission free; ⏱11am-7pm Tue-Thu, noon-8pm Fri-Sun; Ⓜ Şişhane, 🚇 Karaköy, then funicular to Tünel) is housed in a magnificently restored 19th-century building and has an exhibition program featuring big names in the international art world.

☑ Top Tips

▶ Start at Taksim Meydanı and walk down İstiklal before heading through historic Galata to Karaköy, next to the Galata Bridge.

▶ The neighbourhoods within Beyoğlu all have distinct and fascinating characters. Be sure to veer off İstiklal during your perambulation to explore districts such as Cihangir, Çukurcuma and Asmalımescit.

✕ Take a Break

For one of the best Turkish coffees in the city, head to tiny Manda Batmaz (p90), where the *kahveci* (coffee maker) has been perfecting his art for two decades.

Hazzo Pulo Çay Bahçesi (p92) is a popular teahouse hidden in a cobbled courtyard near Galatasaray Meydanı.

Top Sights
İstanbul Modern

In recent years İstanbul's contemporary art scene has boomed. Facilitated by the active cultural philanthropy of the country's industrial dynasties – many of which have built extraordinary arts collections – museum buildings are opening nearly as often as art exhibitions. İstanbul Modern, funded by the Eczcıbaşı family, is the big daddy of them all. Opened with great fanfare in 2005, this huge converted shipping terminal has a stunning location right on the shores of the Bosphorus at Tophane and is easily accessed by tram from Sultanahmet.

İstanbul Modern Sanat Müzesi

◉ Map p84, D6

www.istanbulmodern.org

Meclis-i Mebusan Caddesi

adult/under 12yr ₺17/free

🕙10am-6pm Tue, Wed & Fri-Sun, to 8pm Thu

🚊Tophane

Don't Miss

Downstairs Galleries
The permanent exhibition upstairs is interesting, but the real drawcards at this gallery are the temporary exhibitions on the ground floor. Check out what is showing in the temporary exhibition hall (it's always good), the photography gallery and the pop-up exhibition spaces.

False Ceiling
A visually arresting work by Richard Wentworth, this installation of Turkish and Western books floating overhead plays with ideas of cultural closeness and difference. Created between 1995 and 2005, it dominates the central space downstairs.

Collection Floor
The Eczcıbaşı family's collection of works by prominent 20th-century Turkish artists is showcased on the entrance floor, offering a chronologically organised insight into the country's modern art from its beginnings to the present day.

The Road to Tate Modern
Erkan Özgen and Şener Özmen's 2003 video is an ironic reworking of Cervantes' *Don Quixote*. You'll find it in an upstairs projection room.

Contemporary Showcase
Pieces by high-profile Turkish and international contemporary artists working in the mediums of painting, sculpture, installation and video are exhibited in a small space on the collection floor (next to the restaurant).

☑ **Top Tips**

▶ If your visit coincides with the staging of the İstanbul Biennial (www.iksv.org), check the website for special events and launches.

▶ Book in advance if you plan to have lunch in the restaurant, and specify that you would like a table with a view.

▶ The museum's gift shop stocks jewellery, homewares and stationery made by local artisans and is a good place to source designer souvenirs.

✕ **Take a Break**

The **İstanbul Modern Cafe/Restaurant** (Map p84, D6; ☎212-292 2612; pizzas ₺25-37, pasta ₺25-43, mains ₺37-76; ⊙10am-midnight ; ☑) has a view of the Bosphorus and over to the Historic Peninsula (sometimes obscured by cruise ships, alas) as well as a menu of Italian and Turkish dishes.

Local Life
An Afternoon in and Around Galata

This ancient and highly atmospheric neighbourhood has a very different feel to the rest of the city, perhaps due to its history as a sequestered settlement built and heavily fortified by Genoese traders in the 14th century. Its bohemian credentials are similarly unique, with galleries, bars and boutiques scattered among the handsome apartment buildings that line its narrow cobbled streets.

❶ People-Watching on Galata Meydanı

The square surrounding the Galata Tower is a popular local gathering place. Enjoy a tea with the locals at a square-side cafe while watching young people from across the city congregate on the pavement and outdoor benches surrounding the landmark tower.

Golden Horn (Haliç)

❷ Shopping in Serdar-ı Ekrem Caddesi

One of the city's most interesting and attractive enclaves, this narrow cobbled street is home to highly sought-after apartments as well as boutiques showcasing creations by local designers.

❸ Boho Central

Members of İstanbul's art and fashion communities are regulars at **Mavra** (☏212-252 7488; Serdar-ı Ekrem Caddesi 31a, Galata; breakfast ₺9-27, sandwiches & burgers ₺9-22, pastas ₺15-20; ☺9.30am-2am Mon-Sat, to midnight Sun; Ⓜ Şişhane, Ⓕ Karaköy, then funicular to Tünel), a laid-back cafe with thrift-shop-chic decor.

❹ Designer Wares

Emel Güntaş is one of İstanbul's style icons, and her shop **Hiç** (☏212-251 9973; www.hiccrafts.com; Lüleci Hendek Caddesi 35, Tophane; ☺10.30am-7pm Mon-Sat; Ⓜ Şişhane, Ⓕ Tophane), on the border of Galata and Tophane, is a favourite destination for the city's design mavens. The artisan-made stock includes furniture, cushions, carpets, kilims (pileless woven rugs), silk scarves, porcelain, felt crafts, paintings and photographs.

❺ Camondo Stairs

This sculptural set of stairs is one of Galata's most famous landmarks. Commissioned and paid for by the famous banking family of the same name, it connects Galata with Bankalar Caddesi in Karaköy, which is full of handsome 19th-century bank and insurance-company buildings.

❻ A Cultural Interlude

Housed in a magnificent 1892 bank building designed by Alexandre Vallaury and cleverly adapted by local architectural firm Mimarlar Tasarım, the cutting-edge **SALT Galata** (☏212-334 2200; www.saltonline.org/en; Bankalar Caddesi 11, Karaköy; admission free; ☺noon-8pm Tue-Sat, to 6pm Sun; Ⓕ Karaköy) houses a busy exhibition space and an arts research library used by local curators, students and academics.

❼ Arab Mosque

Built by the Genoese in 1337, this fortress-like building was the largest of İstanbul's Latin churches. Converted to a mosque after the Conquest, it is a popular place of worship for workers in the neighbouring Perşembe Pazarı (literally, 'Thursday Market'), a run-down neighbourhood full of shops selling plumbing and other hardware.

❽ Catch of the Day

Next to the *iskele* (jetty) on the Golden Horn, the small Karaköy Balık Pazarı (Karaköy Fish Market) is a bustling spot where locals shop before hopping on to a ferry to the Asian suburbs. In good weather, the ramshackle but atmospheric fish restaurants next to the market are great places to enjoy a cheap meal.

Gezi
Park
TAKSİM
Taksim
M Funicular
to Kabataş
Osmanlı Sk
Sağnuklu Sk
Sürücüler Sk
Kazancı Başı Camii
Sk
Taksim
Meydanı
Zambak Cad
İstiklal Cad
Bilurcu Sk
Cihangir Cad
Arslan Yatağı Sk
Güneşli Sk
CİHANGİR
Hayriye Sk
Oba Sk
Samanyolu Sk
Susam Sk
Kumrulu Sk
FINDIKLI
İstinaların sefihi

Meşrutiyet Sk
Kurabiye Sk
9
Bekar Sk
32
33
Mis Sk
Küçük Parmak
Kapı Sk
Büyükparmakkapı Hocazade Sk
7
Sadri Alışık
Koca Ağa Sk
39
Nane Sk
Hesnu Galip Sk
Uthis Sk
Mac Sk
Liva Sk
26
21
Soğancı Sk
Sıraselviler Sk
Güllabici Sk
Ağa Hamamı Sk
Yeni Yuva Sk
Akarsu Yokuşu
Bakraç Sk
Palaska Sk
Çukurcuma Sk
Bostanbaşı Cad
23
Kaçatura Sk
Altın Bilezik Sk
Tombak

TARLABAŞI
Taksim Fırını Sk
Tarlabaşı Bul
Sakız Ağacı Cad
Yeşilçam Sk
35
Ayhan Işık Sk
Fatıkza Cad
Hayriye Cad

Halas Sk
Balo Sk
İstiklal
Caddesi
Sahne Sk
Turnacıbaşı Sk
Kartal Sk
14
GALATASARAY
Galatasaray
Lycée
Galatasaray Sk
Yeni Çarşı Cad
BEYOĞLU
Boğazkesen Cad
Tomtom Kaptan Sk
Museum of
Innocence
5

Ömer Hayyam Cad
Arslan Sk
Hamalbaşı Cad
Galatasaray
Meydanı
Tarihi Hazzo
Pulo Pasajı
Akarsu
24
18
Acar Sk
Olivia
Geçidi
Küllav Sk
Eski Çiçekçi Sk
Nuri Ziya Sk
Pera 4
Museum
25
Postacılar Sk
Gönül Sk

Aynalı Çeşme Cad
Işık Çık
Emin Cami Sk
Kasımpaşa
Stadium
Aşıklar Meydanı Sk
Refik Saydam Cad
16
Mesrutiyet Cad
17
Orhan Adli Apaydın Sk
Balyoz Sk
11
12
27
Jurnal Sk
ASMALIMESCİT
Kuyu Sk
Mesrutiyet
Cad
Tepebaşı Cad
Akarca Sk
Şimal Sk
TEPEBAŞI

Meclis-i Mebusan Cad

Senatçılar ...

Bostancı
Cami Sk

Karabaş Cad

Karabaş Deresi Sk

TOPHANE

Tophane İskele Cad

Denizciler

İstanbul Modern

Boşphorus Strait (Boğaziçi)

Fevzi Sk

Kumbaracı Yokuşu

Hacı Mimi Külhanı Sk

Ali Paşa
Medresesi Sk

Tophane Ⓜ

Ali Paşa
Değirmeni Sk

Galeri
Manâ

36 6

Kemankeş Cad

TÜNEL

Şişhane Ⓜ

8 29
34

Şişhane Ⓜ

Tünel Ⓜ
Şişhane Ⓜ

Tünel
Meydanı

38
3
2B

Şahkulu
Bostan Sk

Mevlevi
Museum

Serdar-ı Ekrem Cad

15

Ali Hoca Sk

Hoca Necattey Cad

20 19
Tahsin Sk

22

13

Müeyyethane Cad

Tatlar Beyi Sk

Galipdede Cad

Küçük
Hendek Cad

37

Galata
Tower

2

Galata
Meydanı

30

GALATA

Büyük Hendek Cad

Okçu Musa Cad

Laleli Çeşme Sk

Kuledibi
(Galata Kulesi)
Sk

Bankalar
Cad

GALATA

Lüleci Hendek Cad

Perçemli Sk

Galata

Jewish Museum
of Turkey

1

Arapoğlan Sk

10

KARAKÖY

Gümrük Sk

Karaköy Ⓜ
Tünel (Lower
Station)

Bereketzade
Medresesi Sk

Banker Sk

Bilili Sk

Karaköy Ⓜ

Karaköy
Meydanı

Rıhtım Cad

Karaköy
Balık Pazarı

Kürekçiler Cad

Tersane Cad

Galata
Bridge

Golden Horn (Haliç)

For reviews see

◉	Top Sights	p78
◎	Sights	p86
✕	Eating	p88
⊙	Drinking	p91
✿	Entertainment	p93
⊕	Shopping	p95

200 m
0.1 miles

Sights

Jewish Museum of Turkey

MUSEUM

1 Map p84, B7

Housed in the ornate 19th-century Zullfaris synagogue near the Galata Bridge, this museum was established in 2001 to commemorate the 500th anniversary of the arrival of the Sephardic Jews in the Ottoman Empire. Its modest but extremely well-intentioned collection comprises photographs, papers and objects that document the mostly harmonious coexistence between Jews and the Muslim majority in this country. (500 Yil Vakfi Türk Musevileri, The Quincentennial Foundation Jewish Museum of Turkey; ☑212-244 4474; www.muze500.com; Perçemli Sokak, Karaköy; admission ₺10; ◷10am-4pm Mon-Thu, to 2pm Fri & Sun; ⛴Karaköy)

Galata Tower

TOWER

2 Map p84, A6

The cylindrical Galata Tower stands sentry over the approach to 'new' İstanbul. Constructed in 1348, it was the tallest structure in the city for centuries, and it still dominates the skyline north of the Golden Horn. Its vertiginous upper balcony offers 360-degree views of the city, but we're not convinced that the view (though spectacular) justifies the steep admission cost. (Galata Kulesi; Galata Meydanı, Galata; admission ₺19; ◷9am-8pm; ⛴Karaköy)

Galata Mevlevi Museum

MUSEUM

3 Map p84, B5

The *semahane* (whirling-dervish hall) at the centre of this *tekke* (dervish lodge) was erected in 1491 and renovated in 1608 and 2009. It's part of a complex including a *meydan-ı şerif* (courtyard), *çeşme* (drinking fountain), *türbesi* (tomb) and *hamuşan* (cemetery). The oldest of six historic Mevlevihaneleri (Mevlevi *tekkes*) remaining in İstanbul, the complex was converted into a museum in 1946. (Galata Mevlevihanesi Müzesi; www.mekder. org; Galipdede Caddesi 15, Tünel; admission ₺5; ◷9am-4pm Tue-Sun; Ⓜ Şişhane, ⛴Karaköy, then funicular to Tünel)

Pera Museum

MUSEUM

4 Map p84, B3

Head here to admire works from Suna and İnan Kıraç's splendid collection of paintings featuring Turkish Orientalist themes, which are displayed on the museum's second floor. A changing program of thematic exhibitions drawing on the collection provides fascinating glimpses into the Ottoman world from the 17th to the early 20th century. Some works are realistic, others highly romanticised – all are historically fascinating. (Pera Müzesi; ☑212-334 9900; www.peramuzesi.org.tr; Meşrutiyet Caddesi 65, Tepebaşı; adult/student/child under 12yr ₺15/8/free; ◷10am-7pm Tue-Sat, noon-6pm Sun; Ⓜ Şişhane, ⛴Karaköy, then funicular to Tünel)

Understand
Jewish İstanbul

The history of the Jews in Turkey is as long as it is fascinating. When Mehmet II conquered the city in 1453, he recognised the last Byzantine chief rabbi, Moshe Kapsali, as the chief rabbi of İstanbul and said 'The God has presented me with many lands and ordered me to take care of the dynasty of his servants Abraham and Jacob...Who, among you, with the consent of God, would like to settle in İstanbul, live in peace in the shade of the figs and vineyards, trade freely and own property?' Alas, this enlightened state didn't last through the centuries, and Jewish Turks were made to feel considerably less welcome when racially motivated 'wealth taxes' were introduced in 1942 and violence against Jews and other minorities was unleashed in 1955, prompting many families to flee the country. More recently, Islamist terrorists have bombed synagogues on a number of occasions.

Approximately 23,000 Jews currently live in Turkey, with most residing in İstanbul. Sephardic Jews make up around 96% of this number, while the rest are primarily Ashkenazic. Today there are a total of 16 synagogues in İstanbul, 15 of which are Sephardic. For a list of these see www.jewish-europe.net/turkey/en/synagogue.

Museum of Innocence   MUSEUM

 5 Map p84, C4

The painstaking attention to detail in this fascinating museum/piece of conceptual art will certainly provide every amateur psychologist with a theory or two about its creator, Nobel Prize–winning novelist Orhan Pamuk. Vitrines display a quirky collection of objects that evoke the minutiae of İstanbullu life in the mid-to-late 20th century, when Pamuk's novel of the same name is set. (Masumiyet Müzesi; 212-252 9748; www.masumiyetmuzesi.org, Çukurcuma Caddesi, Dalgıç Çıkmazı, 2; adult/student ₺25/10; 10am-6pm Tue-Sun, to 9pm Thu; M Taksim, Tophane)

Galeri Manâ   GALLERY

6 Map p84, C6

Occupying a converted 19th-century wheat mill in the midst of the city's most happening enclave, Galeri Manâ is perhaps the most interesting of the many commercial galleries to open over the past few years. Its stable of artists includes up-and-coming local and international names such as Abbas Akhavan and Deniz Gül, as well as established practitioners such as Sarkis. (212-243 6666; www.galerimana.com; Ali Paşa Değirmeni Sokak 16-18, Karaköy; 11am-6pm Tue-Sat; Tophane)

Eating

Klemuri ANATOLIAN €€

7 Map p84, D2

The Laz people hail from the Black Sea region, and their cuisine relies heavily on fish, kale and dairy products. One of only a few Laz restaurants in the city, Klemuri serves delicious home-style cooking in bohemian surrounds. There's a well-priced wine list, a dessert *(Laz böreğı)* that has attained a cult following and interesting choices for vegetarians and vegans. (☑212-292 3272; www.klemuri.com; Büyükparmakkapı Sokak 2; starters ₺8-12, mains ₺12-23; ☉noon-11pm Mon-Sat; ☑; MTaksim, ☑Kabataş, then funicular to Taksim)

Antiochia ANATOLIAN €€

8 Map p84, A5

Dishes from the southeastern city of Antakya (Hatay) are the speciality at this foodie destination. Mezes are dominated by wild thyme, pomegranate syrup, olives, walnuts and tangy home-made yoghurt, and the kebaps are equally flavoursome – try the succulent *şiş et* (grilled lamb) or *dürüm* (wrap filled with minced meat, onions and tomatoes). There's a discount at lunch. (☑212-292 1100; www.antiochiaconcept.com; General Yazgan Sokak 3c, Asmalımescit; mezes ₺10-12, mains ₺18-28; ☉lunch Mon-Fri, dinner Mon-Sat; ☑Karaköy, then funicular to Tünel)

Zübeyir Ocakbaşı KEBAPS €€

9 Map p84, D1

Every morning, the chefs at this popular *ocakbaşı* (grill house) prepare the fresh, top-quality meats to be grilled over their handsome copper-hooded barbecues that night: spicy chicken wings and Adana kebaps, flavoursome ribs, pungent liver kebaps and well-marinated lamb *şiş* kebaps. These offerings are famous throughout the city, so booking a table is essential. (☑212-293 3951; Bekar Sokak 28; meze ₺7-9, kebaps ₺22-45; ☉noon-1am; ☑Kabataş, then funicular to Taksim)

Karaköy Güllüoğlu SWEETS, BÖREK €

10 Map p84, C7

This Karaköy institution has been making customers deliriously happy and dentists obscenely rich since 1947. Head to the register and order a *porsiyon* (portion) of whatever baklava takes your fancy (*fıstıklı* is pistachio, *cevizli* walnut and *sade* plain), preferably with a glass of tea. Then hand your ticket over to the servers. The *börek* (filled pastry) here is good, too. (www.karakoygulluoglu.com; Kemankeş Caddesi, Karaköy; portion baklava ₺5-10, portion börek ₺6-7; ☉8am-11pm; ☑Karaköy)

Top Tip

İstanbul Eats

İstanbul Eats (http://istanbuleats.com/) is a popular blog investigating the traditional food culture of the city and is a great resource for those interested in seeking out local eateries and food districts. The team who put it together also conduct excellent culinary walks (p136).

Mezes

Meze by Lemon Tree MODERN TURKISH €€€

11 🍴 Map p84, A4

Chef Gençay Üçok creates some of the most interesting – and delicious – modern Turkish food in the city and serves it in an intimate restaurant opposite the Pera Palace Hotel. We suggest opting for the degustation menu or sticking to the wonderful mezes here rather than ordering mains. Bookings essential. (📞212-252 8302; www.mezze.com.tr; Meşrutiyet Caddesi 83b, Tepebaşı; mezes ₺10-30, 4-course degustation menu for 2 persons ₺160; ⏱7-11pm; 🪑; Ⓜ Şişhane, 🚋 Karaköy, then funicular to Tünel)

Duble Meze Bar MODERN TURKISH €€€

12 🍴 Map p84, A4

Commanding expansive Golden Horn views from its location atop the Palazzo Donizetti Hotel, Duble is an exciting modern take on the traditional *meyhane* experience. On sultry nights, local glamour pusses love nothing better than claiming a designer chair in the glass-sheathed dining space, ordering a cocktail and grazing the menu of 35 different mezes. (📞212-244 0188; www.dublemezebar.com; 7th fl, Meşrutiyet Caddesi 85; cold mezes ₺10-18, hotel mezes ₺16-40; ⏱6pm-2am; 🪑; Ⓜ Şişhane, 🚋 Karaköy, then funicular to Taksim)

Lokanta Maya

MODERN TURKISH €€€

13 Map p84, C7

Critics and chowhounds alike adore the dishes created by chef Didem Şenol at her stylish restaurant near the Karaköy docks. The author of a successful cookbook focusing on Aegean cuisine, Şenol's food is light, flavoursome, occasionally quirky and always assured. You'll need to book for dinner; lunch is cheaper and more casual. (☏212-252 6884; www.lokantamaya.com; Kemankeş Caddesi 35a, Karaköy; starters ₺16-28, mains ₺34-52; ☉noon-5pm & 7-11pm Mon-Sat; ◢; ⛴Karaköy)

Çukur Meyhane

TURKISH €€

14 Map p84, C3

Despite their long and much-vaunted tradition in the city, it is becoming increasingly difficult to find *meyhanes* serving good food. Standards have dropped in many of our old favourites, and we are constantly on the search for replacements. Fortunately, Çukur fits

Local Life

Manda Batmaz

İstanbullus love to sip Cemil Pilik's viscous yet smooth Turkish coffee, and many make a beeline to this tiny **coffee house** (Map p84, B3; Olivia Geçidi 1a, off İstiklal Caddesi; ☉9.30am-midnight; Ⓜ Şişhane, ⛴Karaköy, then funicular to Tünel) whenever they find themselves on İstiklal Caddesi.

the bill. On offer are a convivial atmosphere, great food and relatively cheap prices. Book ahead on weekends. (☏212-244 5575; Kartal Sokak 1; mezes ₺7-16, mains ₺12-17; ☉noon-1am Mon-Sat; ◢; Ⓜ Taksim, ⛴Kabataş, then funicular to Taksim)

Aheste

CAFE €€

15 Map p84, B5

A perfect example of the casual, design-driven cafe model that has been trending in İstanbul over the past few years, Aheste is a small place that's equally alluring for breakfast, morning tea, lunch or dinner. The home-baked cakes and pastries are European-style and delicious, the perfect accompaniment to good Italian-style coffee. Meals are light and packed with flavour. (☏212-245 4345; www.ahestegalata.com; Serdar-ı Ekrem Caddesi 30, Galata; breakfast ₺9-21, soups ₺12-15, sandwiches ₺18-22; ☉9am-midnight; Ⓜ Şişhane, ⛴Karaköy)

Enstitü

CAFE, RESTAURANT €€

16 Map p84, B3

This chic but casual venue would be equally at home in Soho, Seattle or Sydney. A training venue for the **İstanbul Culinary Institute**, it offers freshly baked cakes and pastries, a limited lunch menu that changes daily and a more sophisticated dinner menu that makes full use of seasonal produce. Prices are a steal considering the quality of the food. (www.istanbulculinary.com; Meşrutiyet Caddesi

Bartender at Mikla

59, Tepebaşı; starters ₺10-20, mains ₺15-30; ⊙7.30am-10pm Mon-Fri, 10am-10pm Sat; 🖉; MŞişhane, 🚋Karaköy, then funicular to Tünel)

Drinking

Mikla
BAR

17 📍 Map p84, A4

It's worth overlooking the occasional uppity service at this stylish rooftop bar to enjoy what could well be the best view in İstanbul. After a few drinks, consider moving downstairs to eat in the classy restaurant. (www.miklarestaurant.com; Marmara Pera Hotel,

Meşrutiyet Caddesi 15, Tepebaşı; ⊙from 6pm Mon-Sat summer only; MŞişhane, 🚋Karaköy, then funicular to Tünel)

360
BAR

18 📍 Map p84, B3

This is İstanbul's most famous bar, and deservedly so. If you can score one of the bar stools on the terrace you'll be happy indeed – the view is truly extraordinary. It morphs into a club after midnight on Friday and Saturday, when a cover charge of around ₺40 applies. (www.360istanbul.com; 8th fl, İstiklal Caddesi 163; ⊙noon-2am Sun-Thu, to 4am Fri & Sat; MŞişhane, 🚋Karaköy, then funicular to Tünel)

Karabatak

CAFE

19 Map p84, C6

Hipster central for caffeine fans, Karabatak imports Julius Meinl coffee from Vienna and uses it to conjure up some of the city's best coffee. The outside seating is hotly contested, but the quiet tables inside can be just as alluring. Take your choice from filter, espresso or Turkish brews and order a panino (filled bread roll) or sandwich if you're hungry. (☎212-243 6993; www.karabatak.com; Kara Ali Kaptan Sokak 7, Karaköy; ⏱8.30am-10pm Mon-Fri, 9.30am-10pm Sat & Sun; 🚋Tophane)

Unter

BAR

20 Map p84, C6

This scenester-free zone epitomises the new Karaköy style: it's glam without trying too hard, and has a vaguely arty vibe. The ground-floor windows open to the street in fine weather, allowing the action to spill outside during busy periods. Good cocktails and a wine list strong in boutique Thracian drops are major draws, as is the varied food menu. (☎212 244-5151; http://unter.com.tr; Kara Ali Kaptan Sokak 4, Karaköy; ⏱9am-midnight Tue-Thu & Sun, to 2am Fri & Sat; 🚋Tophane)

MiniMüzikHol

CLUB

21 Map p84, D3

The mothership for innercity hipsters, MMH is a small, slightly grungy venue near Taksim that hosts the best dance party in town on weekends and live sets by local and international musicians midweek. It's best after 1am. (MMH; ☎212-245 1718; www.minimuzikhol.com; Soğancı Sokak 7, Cihangir; ⏱10pm-late Wed-Sat; Ⓜ Taksim, 🚋Kabataş, then funicular to Taksim)

Dem

TEAHOUSE

22 Map p84, C7

We have witnessed long-term expat residents of İstanbul fight back tears as they read the menu at Dem. Their reaction had nothing to do with the price list (which is very reasonable) and everything to do with the joy of choosing from 60 types of freshly brewed tea, all served in fine china cups and with milk on request. (☎212-293 9792; www.demkarakoy.com; Hoca Tahsin Sokak 17, Karaköy; ⏱10am-10pm; 🚋Tophane)

🔍 Local Life

Hazzo Pulo Çay Bahçesi

There aren't as many traditional tea houses in Beyoğlu as there are on the Historic Peninsula, so this **çay bahçesi** (Map p84, B3; Tarihi Hazzo Pulo Pasajı, off İstiklal Caddesi; ⏱9am-midnight; Ⓜ Şişhane, 🚋Karaköy, then funicular to Tünel) in a picturesque cobbled courtyard off İstiklal Caddesi is a local favourite. Order from the waiter and then pay at the small cafe near the narrow arcade entrance.

Cihangir 21 BAR

23 Map p84, D4

The great thing about this neighbourhood place is its inclusiveness – the regulars include black-clad boho types, besuited professionals, expat loafers and quite a few characters who defy categorisation. There's beer on tap (Efes and Miller), a smoker's section and a bustling feel after work hours; it's quite laid-back during the day. (212-251 1626; Coşkun Sokak 21, Cihangir; 9am-2.30am; M Taksim, Kabataş, then funicular to Taksim)

Indigo CLUB

24 Map p84, B3

This is Beyoğlu's electronic music temple and dance-music enthusiasts congregate here on weekends for their energetic kicks. The program spotlights top-notch local and visiting DJs or live acts. (http://indigo-istanbul.com; 1st-5th fl, Mısır Apt, 309 Akarsu Sokak, Galatasaray; 10pm-5am Fri & Sat, closed summer; M Taksim, Kabataş, then funicular to Taksim)

NuTeras BAR, RESTAURANT

25 Map p84, B3

This bar-restaurant attracts a fashionable crowd to the rooftop terrace of the NuPera Building. Its expansive Golden Horn view is spectacular and the after-dinner club scene is trés chic. (www.nupera.com.tr/nuteras; 6th fl, NuPera Bldg, Meşrutiyet Caddesi 67, Tepebaşı; noon-1am Mon-Thu, noon-4am Fri & Sat summer only; M Şişhane, Karaköy, then funicular to Tünel)

Local Life

Tophane Nargile Cafes

This atmospheric row of **nargile cafes** (Map p84, D6; off Necatibey Caddesi, Tophane; 24hr; Tophane) behind the Nusretiye Mosque is always packed with locals enjoying tea, nargile and snacks. Follow your nose to find it – the smell of apple tobacco is incredibly enticing. It costs around ₺50 for a 'VIP package' (tea, one nargile and some snacks to share) or around ₺25 for tea and nargile only.

Kiki BAR, CLUB

26 Map p84, D3

Kiki has a loyal clientele which enjoys its burgers and drinks, but mainly comes for the music (DJs and live sets). Regulars tend to head to the rear courtyard. There's a second branch in Ortaköy (p107). (212-243 5306; www.kiki.com.tr; Sıraselviler Caddesi 42, Cihangir; 6pm-2am Mon-Wed, to 4am Thu-Sat; M Taksim, Kabataş, then funicular to Taksim)

Entertainment

Babylon LIVE MUSIC, CLUB

27 Map p84, A4

İstanbul's pre-eminent live-music venue has been packing the crowds in since 1999 and shows no sign of losing its mojo. The eclectic program often features big-name international music

Local Life

Türkü Evleri

Hasnun Galip Sokak in Galatasaray is home to a number of *Türkü evleri*, Kurdish-owned bars where musicians perform live, emotion-charged *halk meziği* (folk music) in front of groups of locals who sing along with gusto. Venues such as **Munzur Cafe & Bar** (Map p84, D2; ☎212-245 4669; www.munzurcafebar.com; Hasnun Galip Sokak 17, Galatasaray; ⏰1pm-4am, music from 9pm; Ⓜ Taksim, 🚋 Kabataş, then funicular to Taksim) are particularly busy on Friday and Saturday nights.

acts, particularly during the festival season. Most of the action occurs in the club, but there's also a lounge with a DJ; access this from Jurnal Sokak. (www.babylon.com.tr; Şehbender Sokak 3, Asmalımescit; ⏰lounge from 5pm, club from 8.30pm Tue-Thu, from 10.30pm Fri & Sat, closed summer; Ⓜ Şişhane, 🚋 Karaköy, then funicular to Tünel)

Galata Mevlevi Museum

PERFORMING ARTS

28 ★ Map p84, B5

The 15th-century *semahane* (whirling-dervish hall) at this *tekke* (dervish lodge) is the venue for a *sema* (ceremony) held on Saturdays and Sundays during the year. Come early (preferably days ahead) to buy your ticket. (Galata Mevlevihanesi Müzesi; Galipdede Caddesi 15, Tünel; ₺40; ⏰performances 5pm Sat & Sun; 🚋 Karaköy, then funicular to Tünel)

Salon

LIVE MUSIC

29 ★ Map p84, A5

This intimate performance space in the İstanbul Foundation for Culture & Arts (İKSV) building hosts live contemporary music (classical, jazz, rock, alternative and world music) as well as theatrical and dance performances; check the website for program and booking details. Before or after the show, consider having a drink at **X Bar**, in the same building. (☎212-334 0752; www.saloniksv.com; ground fl, İstanbul Foundation for Culture & Arts, Sadi Konuralp Caddesi 5, Şişhane; ⏰Oct-May; Ⓜ Şişhane, 🚋 Karaköy, then funicular to Tünel)

Nardis Jazz Club

JAZZ

30 ★ Map p84, A6

Named after a Miles Davis track, this intimate venue near the Galata Tower is run by jazz guitarist Önder Focan and his wife Zuhal. Performers include gifted amateurs, local jazz luminaries and visiting international artists. It's small, so you'll need to book if you want a decent table. (☎212-244 6327; www.nardisjazz.com; Kuledibi Sokak 14, Galata; ⏰9.30pm-12.30am Mon-Thu, 10.30pm-1.30am Fri & Sat, closed Aug; Ⓜ Şişhane, 🚋 Karaköy)

Nublu İstanbul

JAZZ

31 ★ Map p84, B7

This ultra-cool basement venue in the Gradiva Hotel is run by – or at least in association with – New York–based jazz saxophonist and composer, İlhan

SALVATOR BARKI/GETTY IMAGES ©

Whirling dervishes

Ersahin. It closes during summer, but has a busy and never predictable program for the rest of the year. Check the club's website or Facebook page for what's on. (☎212-249 7712; www. nubluistanbul.net; Gravida Hotel, Voyvoda Sokak 2/1, Karaköy; ⊗10pm-3am Wed-Sun Oct-May; ☒Karaköy)

Shopping

Nahıl   HANDICRAFTS, BATHWARE

32 🔒 Map p84, D1

The felting, lacework, embroidery, all-natural soaps and soft toys in this lovely shop are made by economically disadvantaged women in Turkey's rural areas and all profits are returned to them, ensuring that they and their families have better lives. (☎212-251 9085; www.nahil.com.tr; Bekar Sokak 17; ⊗10am-7pm Mon-Sat; MTaksim, ☒Kabataş, then funicular to Taksim)

Beyoğlu Olgunlaşma Enstıtüsü   HANDICRAFTS

33 🔒 Map p84, D2

This is the ground-floor retail outlet-gallery of the Beyoğlu Olgunlaşma Enstıtüsü, a textile school where students in their final year of secondary school learn crafts such as felting, embroidery, knitting and lacemaking. It sells well-priced examples of their work, giving them a taste of its commercial possibilities.

İKSV Tasarım Mağazası

(www.beyogluolgunlasma.k12.tr; İstiklal Caddesi 28; ⊘9am-5pm Mon-Fri; Ⓜ Taksim, 🚋 Kabataş, then funicular to Taksim)

İKSV Tasarım Mağazası
JEWELLERY, HOMEWARES

34 🅰 Map p84, A5

A secret to sourcing a great souvenir of your trip to İstanbul? Ignore the mass-produced junk sold in many shops around the city and instead head to a museum or gallery store like this one. Run by the İstanbul Foundation for Culture & Arts (İKSV), it sells jewellery, ceramics and glassware designed and made by local artisans. (İKSV Gift Shop; 🖉 212-334 0830; www. iksvtasarim.com; İstanbul Foundation for Culture & Arts, Sadi Konuralp Caddesi 5, Şişhane; ⊘10am-7pm Mon-Sat; Ⓜ Şişhane, 🚋 Karaköy, then funicular to Tünel)

A La Turca
CARPETS, ANTIQUES

35 🅰 Map p84, D3

Antique Anatolian kilims and textiles are stacked alongside top-drawer Ottoman antiques in this fabulous shop in Çukurcuma. This is the best area in the city to browse for antiques and curios, and A La Turca is probably the most interesting of its retail outlets. Ring the doorbell to gain entrance. (🖉 212-245 2933; www.alaturca-house.com; Faikpaşa Sokak 4, Çukurcuma; ⊘10.30am-7.30pm Mon-Sat; Ⓜ Taksim, 🚋 Kabataş, then funicular to Taksim)

Selda Okutan   JEWELLERY

36 🔒 Map p84, C6

Selda Okutan's sculptural pieces, featuring tiny naked figures, have the local fashion industry all aflutter. Come to her design studio in Tophane to see what the fuss is about. (📞 212-514 1164; www.seldaokutan.com; Ali Paşa Değirmeni Sokak 10a, Tophane; ⏱closed Sun; 🚋Tophane)

Old Sandal   SHOES

37 🔒 Map p84, B6

Owning a pair of Hülya Samancı's handmade shoes, boots or sandals is high on many local wishlists. Pop into this tiny store in the shadow of the Galata Tower to admire these 100% leather creations for men and women. (📞 212-292 8647; www.oldsandal.com.tr; Serdar-ı Ekrem Sokak 10a, Galata; ⏱11am-7.30pm; 🅼Şişhane, 🚋Karaköy, then funicular to Tünel)

Lale Plak   MUSIC

38 🔒 Map p84, B5

This small shop is crammed with CDs, including a fine selection of Turkish classical, jazz and folk music. It's a popular hang-out for local musicians. (📞 212-293 7739; Galipdede Caddesi 1, Tünel; ⏱noon-7pm; 🅼Şişhane, 🚋Karaköy, then funicular to Tünel)

Ali Muhıddin Hacı Bekir   FOOD & DRINK

39 🔒 Map p84, D2

The Beyoğlu branch of the famous *lokum* (Turkish delight) shop. (📞 212-244 2804; www.hacibekir.com.tr; İstiklal Caddesi 83; 🅼Taksim, 🚋Kabataş, then funicular to Taksim Meydanı)

Explore

Dolmabahçe Palace & Ortaköy

The stretch of Bosphorus shore between Beşiktaş and Ortaköy is home to the splendid Ottoman-era buildings of Dolmabahçe, Yıldız and Çırağan. North of this picturesque palace precinct is the famous 'Golden Mile', a string of upmarket nightclubs running between the waterside suburbs of Ortaköy and Kuruçeşme, once humble fishing villages and now prime pockets of real estate.

The Sights in a Day

Beat the queues by arriving at **Dolmabahçe Palace** (p100) as soon as it opens. After taking the compulsory guided tour and visiting the **National Palaces Painting Museum** (p101), enjoy a tea at the waterside *çay bahçesi* (tea garden) and then catch a bus or taxi to Ortaköy for lunch at **Banyan** (p106) or **Zuma** (p106).

Those who haven't yet reached Ottoman overload could then head to **Yıldız Park** (p105) to visit the chalet built by order of Sultan Abdül Hamit II. Alternatively, the impressive new wing of the **İstanbul Naval Museum** (p105) showcases a spectacular collection of imperial caïques (ornately decorated wooden rowboats). Afterwards, consider having a drink on the terrace of the **Çırağan Palace Kempinski Hotel** (p107).

After dinner at **Vogue** (p106), kick on to party with the glitterati against the illuminated backdrop of the monumental Bosphorus Bridge at **Reina** (p107) or **Sortie** (p107).

For a local's day in Ortaköy, see p102.

⊙ Top Sights
Dolmabahçe Palace (p100)

◯ Local Life
Weekend Wander in Ortaköy (p102)

♥ Best of İstanbul
Architecture
Dolmabahçe Palace (p100)

Çırağan Palace (p106)

Museums & Galleries
National Palaces Painting Museum (p101)

İstanbul Naval Museum (p105)

Nightlife
Reina (p107)

Sortie (p107)

Getting There

🚌 **Bus** Lines 22, 22RE and 25E travel from Kabataş along Çırağan, Muallim Naci and Kuruçeşme Caddesis and on to the Bosphorus suburbs. Lines 40, 40T or 42T travel from Taksim.

⛴ **Ferry** Commuter ferries run from Eminönü to Ortaköy in the early evening on weekdays, but there are no return services.

Top Sights
Dolmabahçe Palace

These days it's fashionable for critics influenced by the less-is-more aesthetic of the Bauhaus masters to sneer at buildings such as Dolmabahçe. Enthusiasts of Ottoman architecture also decry this final flourish of the imperial dynasty, dismissing it as vulgarly ostentatious. But whatever the critics might say, this 19th-century palace with its magnificent Bosphorus location, formal garden, opulent Selâmlık (State or Ceremonial Apartments) and large Harem is a clear crowd favourite.

◉ Map p18, A4

www.millisaraylar.gov.tr

Dolmabahçe Caddesi

adult Selâmlık ₺30, Harem ₺20, under 7yr free

🕑9am-3.30pm Tue, Wed & Fri-Sun Apr-Oct, to 2.30pm Nov-Mar

🚋Kabataş then walk

Don't Miss

Imperial Selâmlık

The palace's state apartments were decorated by Frenchman Charles Séchan, designer of the Paris Opera, and are highly theatrical in appearance. They feature a crystal staircase manufactured by Baccarat, mirrored fireplaces, parquet floors, and Sèvres and Yıldız (locally made) porcelain. The most impressive room is the huge Muayede Salon (Ceremonial Hall), which features a purpose-woven 124-sq-metre Hereke carpet and a crystal chandelier weighing 4.5 tonnes.

Imperial Harem

Decoration of the Harem is relatively restrained by Dolmabahçe standards (which isn't saying much). Its most notable elements are the hand-painted ceilings, which feature throughout. The tour passes bedrooms, private salons, a circumcision room and a nursery.

Atatürk's Deathbed

Dolmabahçe was used by the first president of the Republic when he visited İstanbul, and he died here on 10 November 1938. The Harem tour pauses at his bedroom, which features a bed draped in the Turkish flag and a clock stopped at 9.05am, when the great man drew his last breath.

National Palaces Painting Museum

Reopened in 2014 after a long restoration, the Veliaht Dairesi (Apartments of the Crown Prince) now showcase the palace's collection of paintings in the **National Palaces Painting Museum** (Milli Saraylar Resim Müzesi; ⊙9am-4pm Tue, Wed & Fri-Sun). Highlights include the downstairs 'Turkish Painters 1870–1890' room, which includes two Osman Hamdi Bey works, and the upstairs 'İstanbul views' room, which is home to 19th-century street scenes by Germain Fabius Brest.

☑ Top Tips

▶ Visitor numbers in the palace are limited to 3000 per day and this ceiling is often reached on weekends and holidays – come midweek if possible, and even then be prepared to queue (often for a long period and in full sun).

▶ Entry to the National Palaces Painting Museum housed in the Apartments of the Crown Prince behind the Harem is included in the ticket price.

▶ If you arrive before 3pm in summer or 2pm in winter, you must buy a combined ticket to tour both the Selâmlık and Harem; after those times you can take only one tour (we recommend opting for the Selâmlık).

✖ Take a Break

There's a çay bahçesi near the clock tower with premium Bosphorus views and bargain prices (yes, really).

Local Life
Weekend Wander in Ortaköy

The settlement of Ortaköy (Turkish for 'Middle Village') dates back to Byzantine times, when it was a small fishing village. These days the picturesque cobbled laneways surrounding its waterside square, known as İskele (Ferry Dock) Meydanı, are filled with cafes, bars and fast-food stands. On Sundays a handicrafts market draws visitors from across the city.

1 İskele Meydanı

Locals love to promenade around this attractive square, which fronts the water and has a backdrop of old timber houses now functioning as restaurants and cafes. In its centre is a pretty 18th-century *çeşme* (fountain). On Sundays the streets surrounding the square are crowded with market stalls selling handicrafts. Cheap imports from the Subcontinent and China

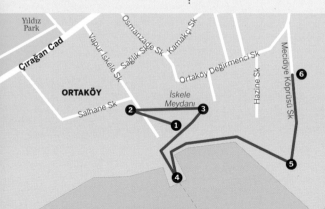

predominate, but some stalls sell handicrafts made by local artisans.

❷ Brunch at the House Cafe

İstanbullus love to brunch, especially if they can do so in glamorous surrounds. The Ortaköy branch of the chic **House Cafe** (İskele Meydanı 42; breakfast platters ₺24, sandwiches ₺15-26, pizzas ₺17.50-27.50, mains ₺16.50-29.50; ⓢ9am-1am Mon-Thu, to 2am Fri & Sat, to 10.30pm Sun; 🚇Kabataş Lisesi) has a million-lira location right on the water's edge and is hugely popular with locals on weekends.

❸ Sampling Dondurma

Originating in the southeastern region of Maraş, *dondurma* (Turkish ice cream) is made with salep (ground dried orchid root) and mastic (pine-flavoured resin from the mastic tree) as well as milk and sugar. These unusual ingredients give the ice cream a distinctive chewy texture. Sample some at one of the cafes on or around İskele Meydanı.

❹ Bosphorus Tour

Most tourists take a crowded excursion ferry at Eminönü to cruise the Bosphorus, but if you're here in the afternoon, consider hopping aboard İstanbul Şehir Hatları's Short Bosphorus Tour, which departs from Eminönü and takes passengers aboard at the Ortaköy *iskele* (ferry dock) at 2.50pm daily for a 1½-hour cruise up to İstinye and back.

❺ A Perfect Photo Opportunity

With the modern Bosphorus Bridge looming behind it, the 19th-century baroque-style **Ortaköy Mosque** provides a fabulous photo opportunity for those wanting to illustrate İstanbul's 'old meets new' character. The elegant mosque was designed by Nikoğos Balyan, one of the architects of Dolmabahçe Palace, and built for Sultan Abdül Mecit I between 1853 and 1855. In the light and airy interior, look for several masterful examples of Arabic calligraphy executed by Abdül Mecit, who was an accomplished calligrapher.

❻ Kümpir & Waffle Stands

The pedestrianised street behind the mosque is crowded with stands selling *kümpir* (stuffed baked potato) and sweet-smelling waffles. Either makes a perfect mid-afternoon snack.

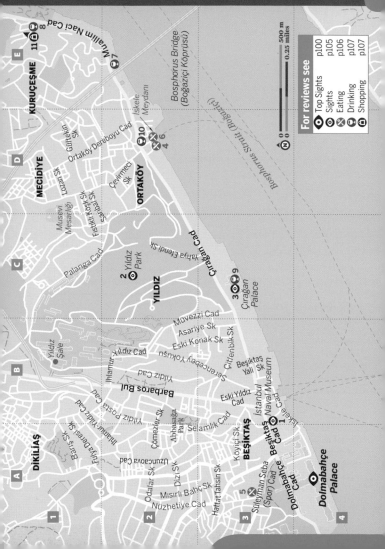

Muallim Naci Cad

KURUÇEŞME

MECİDİYE

Ortaköy Dereboyu Cad

İskele Meydanı

Bosphorus Bridge
(Boğaziçi Köprüsü)

ORTAKÖY

Gültekin Sk

Lozan Sk

Çevirmeci Sk

Müsevi Mesarığı

Fıstıklı Köşk Sk

Salpa Sk

Palanga Cad

Bosphorus Strait (Boğaziçi)

YILDIZ

Yıldız Park

Yahya Efendi Sk

Çırağan Cad

Çırağan Palace

Muvezzi Cad

Asariye Sk

Eski Konak Sk

Yıldız Yolu Cad

İhlamur

Çitlenbik Sk

Beşiktaş Yalı Sk

Serencebey Yokuşu

Yıldız Şale

Yıldız Cad

Barbaros Bul

Eski Yıldız Cad

İstanbul Naval Museum

DİKİLİTAŞ

Baruş Sk

Fulya Deresi Sk

İhlamur Yıldız Cad

Yıldız Posta Cad

Çömezler Sk

Abbasağa Park

Selamlık Cad

Köyiçi Sk

İskele Cad

BEŞİKTAŞ

Uzunçeova Cad

Dizi Sk

Odalar Sk

Mısırlı Bahçe Sk

Hattat Tahsin Sk

Süleyman Seba (Spor) Cad

Nüzhetiye Cad

Beşiktaş Cad

Dolmabahçe Cad

Dolmabahçe Palace

0   500 m
0   0.25 miles

Çırağan Palace (p106)

Sights

İstanbul Naval Museum   MUSEUM

1 ◎ Map p104, B3

Established more than a century ago to celebrate and commemorate Turkish naval history, this museum has recently been undergoing a prolonged and major renovation. Its architecturally noteworthy copper-clad exhibition hall opened in 2013 and showcases a spectacular collection of 19th-century imperial caïques, ornately decorated wooden rowboats used by the royal household. Exhibits about naval battles are located in a downstairs gallery, as is part of the chain that stretched across the Golden Horn during Mehmet the Conqueror's assault on Constantinople. (İstanbul Deniz Müzesi; ☑212-327 4345; www.denizmuzeleri.tsk.tr, Beşiktaş Caddesi 6, Beşiktaş; adult/student & child ₺6/free; ⊙9am-5pm Tue-Sun Oct–mid-Apr, 9am-5pm Tue-Fri & 10am-6pm Sat & Sun mid-Apr–Sep; ☒Bahçeşehir Unv)

Yıldız Park   PARK

2 ◎ Map p104, C2

This large and leafy retreat is alive with birds, picnicking families and young couples enjoying a bit of hanky-panky in the bushes. At its highest point is a **şale** (Yıldız Chalet Museum; Map p104; ☑212-259 4570; www.millisaraylar.gov. tr; adult/child ₺10/5; ⊙9am-4.30pm Tue-Wed & Fri-Sun Apr-Oct, to 3.30pm Nov-Mar), or chalet, commissioned by Sultan Abdül Hamit II as a hunting lodge. Built in 1880, this was converted into a guesthouse for visiting foreign dignitaries in 1889 and is now a museum. The best time to visit the park is in April, when its spring flowers (including thousands of tulips) bloom. (Yıldız Parkı; Çırağan Caddesi, Yıldız; Yahya Efendi)

Çırağan Palace

PALACE

3 Map p104, C3

Not satisfied with the architectural exertions of his predecessor at Dolmabahçe, Sultan Abdül Aziz (r 1861–76) built his own grand residence at Çırağan, only 1.5km away. Here, architect Nikoğos Balyan, who had also worked on Dolmabahçe, created an interesting building melding European neoclassical with Ottoman and Moorish styles. The palace is now part of the Çırağan Palace Kempinski Hotel. (Çırağan Sarayı; Çırağan Caddesi 84, Ortaköy; Çırağan)

Eating

Zuma

JAPANESE €€€

4 Map p104, D2

Izakaya-style dishes from the robata grill and raw treats from the sushi bar draw a loyal crew of locals to this branch of the popular London restaurant, but the main draw is the amazing waterside location. There's also a sake bar and lounge on the top floor. (☑212-236 2296; www.zumarestaurant.com; Salhane Sokak 7, Ortaköy; mains ₺50-100; ⏱lunch from noon Mon-Fri, 1pm Sat & Sun, dinner from 7pm daily; 🖊; Kabataş Lisesi)

Vogue

INTERNATIONAL €€€

5 Map p104, A3

It seems as if Vogue has been around for almost as long as the Republic. In fact, this sophisticated bar-restaurant in an office block in Beşiktaş opened more than a decade ago. It's a favourite haunt of the Nişantaşı powerbroker set, who like to have a drink at the terrace bar before moving into the restaurant for dinner. (☑212-227 4404; www.voguerestaurant.com; 13th fl, A Blok, BJK Plaza, Spor Caddesi 92, Akaretler, Beşiktaş; starters ₺26-50, mains ₺30-75; ⏱noon-2am Mon-Sat, 10.30am-2am Sun; 🖊; Akaretler)

Banyan

ASIAN €€€

6 Map p104, D2

The menu here travels around Asia, featuring Thai, Japanese, Indian, Vietnamese and Chinese dishes including soups, sushi, satays and salads. The food claims to be good for the soul, and you can enjoy it while revelling in the exceptional views of the Ortaköy Mosque and Bosphorus Bridge from the terrace. There's a 10% discount at lunch. (☑212-259 9060; www.banyanrestaurant.com; 3rd fl, Salhane Sokak 3, Ortaköy; starters ₺14-39, sushi rolls ₺18-29, mains ₺30-85; ⏱noon-midnight; 🖊; Kabataş Lisesi)

Drinking

Reina
CLUB

7 Map p104, E2

According to its website, Reina is where 'foreign heads of state discuss world affairs, business people sign agreements of hundred billions of dollars and world stars visit'. In reality, it's where Turkey's C-list celebrities congregate, the city's nouveaux riches flock and an occasional tourist gets past the doorman to ogle the spectacle. The Bosphorus location is truly extraordinary. (212-259 5919; www.reina.com.tr; Muallim Naci Caddesi 44, Ortaköy; Ortaköy)

Sortie
CLUB

8 Map p104, E1

Sortie has long vied with Reina for the title of reigning queen of the Golden Mile, nipping at the heels of its rival dowager. It pulls in the city's glamour-pusses and poseurs, all of whom are on the lookout for the odd celebrity guest. (212-327 8585; www.sortie.com.tr; Muallim Naci Caddesi 54, Kuruçeşme; Şifa Yurdu)

Çırağan Palace Kempinski Hotel
BAR

9 Map p104, C3

Nursing a mega-pricey drink or coffee at one of the Çırağan's terrace tables and watching the scene around the city's best swimming pool, which is right on the Bosphorus, lets you sample the lifestyle of the city's rich and famous. (212-326 4646; www.clragan-palace.com; Çırağan Caddesi 32, Ortaköy; Çırağan)

Kiki
BAR, CLUB

10 Map p104, D2

An Ortaköy offshoot of the popular Cihangir venue. (212-258 5524; http://kiki.com.tr; Osmanzade Sok 8, Ortaköy; 5pm-1am Tue-Fri, to 5am Fri & Sat, to midnight Sun)

Shopping

Lokum
FOOD

11 Map p104, E1

Lokum (Turkish delight) is elevated to the status of artwork at this boutique on the border of Kuruçeşme and Arnavutköy. Owner/creator Zeynep Keyman aims to bring back the delights, flavours, knowledge and beauty of Ottoman-Turkish products such as *lokum, akide* candies (traditional boiled lollies), cologne water and scented candles. The gorgeous packaging makes these treats perfect gifts. (212-287 1528; www.lokumistanbul.com; Arnavutköy-Bebek Caddesi 15, Arnavutköy; 9am-7pm Mon-Sat; Arnavutköy)

Top Sights
The Bosphorus

Getting There

⛴ Full-day tour (one way/return ₺15/25, six hours) departs Eminönü daily at 10.35am; extra service at 1.35pm from April to October. Short tours (₺10 to ₺12, 90 minutes) depart Eminönü daily.

This mighty strait runs from the Galata Bridge 32km north to the Black Sea (Karadeniz). Over the centuries it has been crossed by conquering armies, intrepid merchants, fishermen and many an adventurous spirit. To follow in their wake, hop aboard a ferry cruise. Along the way, you'll see magnificent *yalıs* (waterside timber mansions), ornate Ottoman palaces and massive stone fortresses that line the Asian and European shores (to your right and left, respectively, as you sail down the strait).

View of the Bosphorus and Ortaköy Mosque

Don't Miss

Dolmabahçe & Çırağan Palaces

As the ferry starts its journey from Eminönü, look for the 18th-century tower of **Kız Kulesi** on a tiny island just off the Asian shore. Just before Beşiktaş, on the European shore, you'll pass grandiose Dolmabahçe Palace (p100). After a brief stop at Beşiktaş, the ferry passes ornate Çırağan Palace (p106), which is now a luxury hotel. Next to it is a long yellow building occupied by Galatasaray University.

Yalıs

Both sides of the Bosphorus shore are lined with *yalıs* (timber waterside mansions) built by Ottoman aristocracy and foreign ambassadors in the 17th, 18th and 19th centuries. They are now the most prestigious addresses in town, owned by industrialists, bankers and media tycoons.

Ortaköy Mosque

The dome and two minarets of this 19th-century mosque on the European shore are dwarfed by the adjacent **Bosphorus Bridge**, which was opened in 1973 on the 50th anniversary of the founding of the Turkish Republic.

Beylerbeyi Palace

This 26-room baroque-style **palace** (Beylerbeyi Sarayı; www.millisaraylar.gov.tr; Abdullah Ağa Caddesi, Beylerbeyi; adult/student/child under 7yr ₺20/₺5/free; ⊙9am-4.30pm Tue, Wed & Fri-Sun Apr-Oct, to 3.30pm Nov-Mar; ⊒Beylerbeyi Sarayı) on the Asian shore was built for Abdül Aziz I. Look for its whimsical marble bathing pavilions; one was for men, the other for the women of the Harem.

Bebek

This upmarket suburb is known for its fashion boutiques and chic cafes. As the ferry passes,

---

☑ **Top Tips**

▶ The full-day tour involves a three-hour stop in the tourist-trap village of Anadolu Kavağı. Instead, buy a one-way ticket and return on bus 15A, stopping at Kanlıca to visit Hıdiv Kasrı and then transferring to bus 15 for Üsküdar via Küçüksu Kasrı and Beylerbeyi Palace. For timetables see www.iett.gov.tr/en.

▶ If you're keen to visit Ottoman heritage, a hop-on/hop-off ferry service (www.denturavrasya.com) departs from behind the petrol station at Kabataş at 12.45pm, 1.45pm, 2.45pm, 3.45pm, 4.45pm and 5.45pm daily (₺15) stopping at Küçüksu Kasrı and Beylerbeyi Sarayı.

✗ **Take a Break**

There's a glamorous restaurant with a terrace overlooking the Bosphorus in the Sakıp Sabancı Museum, and both Hıdiv Kasrı and Beylerbeyi Palace have charming garden cafes.

look for the Ottoman Revivalist–style **Bebek Mosque** and the art nouveau **Egyptian consulate** building with its mansard roof.

Küçüksu Kasrı

This ornate **hunting lodge** (☑216-332 3303; Küçüksu Caddesi, Beykoz; adult/student/child under 7yr ₺5/1/free; ⊙9am-4.30pm Tue, Wed & Fri-Sun Apr-Oct, to 3.30pm Nov-Mar; ◻Küçüksu) on the Asian shore was built for Sultan Abdül Mecit in 1856–7. Earlier sultans used wooden kiosks here, but architect Nikoğos Balyan designed a rococo gem in marble for his monarch.

Rumeli Hisarı

Just before the Fatih Bridge is the majestic **Rumeli Hisarı** (Fortress of Europe; ☑212-263 5305; Yahya Kemal Caddesi 42; admission ₺10; ⊙9am-noon & 12.30-4.30pm Thu-Tue; ◻Rumeli Hisarı), built by order of Mehmet the Conqueror in preparation for his siege of Byzantine Constantinople. For its location, he chose the narrowest point of the Bosphorus, opposite **Anadolu Hisarı** (Fortress of Asia), which Sultan Beyazıt I had built in 1391.

Anadolu Hisarı

There are many architecturally and historically important *yalıs* in and around the village of Anadolu Hisarı. These include the **Zarif Mustafa Paşa Yalı**, built in the early 19th century by the official coffee maker to Sultan Mahmud II. Look for its upstairs salon, which juts out over the water and is supported by unusual curved timber struts.

Kanlıca

Past the bridge on the Asian side is Kanlıca, the ferry's second stop. It's famous for the rich and delicious yoghurt produced here, which is sold on the ferry and in two cafes on the shady waterfront square.

Hıdiv Kasrı

High on a promontory above Kanlıca is this gorgeous **art nouveau villa** (Khedive's Villa; www.beltur.com.tr; Çubuklu Yolu 32, Çubuklu; admission free; ⊙9am-10pm; ⛴Kanlıca), built by the last Khedive of Egypt as a summer residence for his family.

Emirgan

On the opposite shore is the wealthy suburb of Emirgan, home to the impressive **Sakıp Sabancı Museum** (Sakıp Sabancı Müzesi; ☑212-277 2200; http://muze.sabanciuniv.edu; Sakıp Sabancı Caddesi 42, Emirgan; adult/student/child under 8yr ₺15/8/free; ⊙10am-5.30pm Tue, Thu & Fri-Sun, to 7.30pm Wed; ◻Emirgan), which hosts international travelling art exhibitions.

Sarıyer

The ferry's third stop is Sarıyer, on the European shore. Its residents have traditionally made a living by fishing, and the area around the ferry terminal is full of fish restaurants.

Anadolu Kavağı

This village on the Asian shore is the ferry's last stop. Its economy was built on the fishing trade, but today it relies more on tourism. The main square is full of mediocre fish restaurants.

The Best of
İstanbul

Wares for sale in the Grand Bazaar (p56)
MATT MUNRO/LONELY PLANET ©

Best Walks
Sultanahmet Saunter

🏃 The Walk

Despite spending the majority of their time in or around Sultanahmet, most visitors see little of this historic district other than their hotel and the major monuments. This walk will take you off the well-worn tourist routes and introduce some lesser-known Ottoman and Byzantine sights.

Start Sultanahmet Park; 🚋Sultanahmet

Finish Arasta Bazaar; 🚋Sultanahmet

Length 2.3km; two hours

✕ Take a Break

There are plenty of tea and coffee options in this area, but few are as atmospheric as the Caferağa Medresesi Çay Bahçesi (p53), set in the tranquil courtyard of the historic *medrese* (theological school) of the same name.

Arasta Bazaar

① Aya Sofya Tombs

Start the walk at Aya Sofya Meydanı (Aya Sofya Sq), turning left into Kabasakal Caddesi to visit these splendid Ottoman tombs (p33), the final resting places of five sultans.

② Fountain of Sultan Ahmet III

This exquisite rococo-style fountain kiosk (1728) outside Topkapı Palace once dispensed cold drinks of water and *şerbet* (sweet cordial) to thirsty travellers.

③ Soğukçeşme Sokak

Veer down this picturesque cobbled street (p49), which is home to re-created Ottoman timber houses and a restored Byzantine cistern.

④ Caferağa Medresesi

Turn left into Caferiye Sokak to visit this lovely little medrese (theological school) tucked away in the shadows of Aya Sofya. Commissioned by Süleyman the Magnificent's chief black eunuch, it was built in

KORHAN SEZER/GETTY IMAGES ©

1560 and is now home to an organisation supporting traditional handicrafts.

5 Sokollu Şehit Mehmet Paşa Mosque

Head towards busy Alemdar Caddesi and then veer left to reach the Hippodrome (p33). Walk its length and then into Şehit Mehmet Paşa Yokuşu. Continue down Katip Sinan Cami Sokak until you reach this splendid Ottoman-era mosque, which has an interior adorned with fine İznik tiles.

6 Little Aya Sofya

Veer left down Şehit Çeşmesi Sokak, then turn left into Kadırga Limanı Caddesi and you'll soon arrive at Küçük Ayasofya Caddesi, home to Little Aya Sofya (p35), one of the most beautiful Byzantine buildings in the city.

7 Sphendone

Walk east along Küçük Ayasofya Caddesi and continue left up the hill at Aksakal Caddesi. At the crest is the only remaining built section of the Hippodrome, the Sphendone. Opposite is a huge carpet shop called Nakkaş that has a restored Byzantine cistern in its basement.

8 Arasta Bazaar

Continue along Nakilbent Sokak, then veer right down Şifa Hamamı Sokak, turning left into Küçük Ayasofya Caddesi and continuing straight ahead to the Arasta Bazaar, a historic row of shops once part of the Blue Mosque *külliye* (mosque complex).

Best Walks
Ottoman Old City

🏃 The Walk

In the Ottoman era, the narrow streets surrounding the Süleymaniye Mosque were full of timber mansions built by wealthy merchants, high-ranking soldiers and court dignitaries. This walk will take you onto their home turf, passing historically significant building stock that is slowly being restored as part of the Süleymaniye Urban Regeneration Project.

Start Süleymaniye Mosque; 🚋Laleli-Üniversite

Finish Kadınlar Pazarı; 🚋Zeyrek

Length 2km; two hours

🍴 Take A Break

Locals swear by the energising properties of *boza*, a viscous drink made from water, sugar and fermented barley, and head to historic Vefa Bozacısı (p70) for regular fixes during the cooler months.

KORHAN SEZER/GETTY IMAGES ©

❶ Tiryaki Çarşısı

Start in the street fronting the Süleymaniye Mosque (p60). This was once known as the 'Street of the Addicts' due to its preponderance of tea houses selling opium, but is now home to *fasulyecıs* (bean restaurants) popular with students from nearby İstanbul University and with worshippers from the mosque.

❷ Kayserili Ahmet Paşa Konağı

Head down narrow Ayşekadin Hamamı Sokak (look for the 'Süleymaniye Kütüphanesi' sign in the middle of the souvenir stands) and you will eventually come to this pretty three-storey mansion, once home to a minister of the Ottoman navy and now the headquarters of the city's Directorate of Inspection of Conservation Implementation.

❸ Ekmekçizade Ahmetpaşa Medresesi

Continue along Kayserili Ahmetpaşa Sokak and then veer right, passing a football pitch, until you come to this medrese, built between 1603–17 by the son of a baker from Edirne who rose up the ranks of Ottoman society to became a *defterder* (first lord of the treasury).

4 Şehzade Mehmet Mosque

From the *medrese*, turn right into Cemal Yener Tosyalı Caddesi and then left into Şehzade Camii Sokak. Pass under the stone arch to reach the rear gate of this elegant mosque, built by order of Süleyman the Magnificent as a memorial to his son, Mehmet, who died of smallpox in 1543 at the age of 22.

5 Fatih Anıt Park

After visiting the mosque, head west; you'll see remnants of the majestic Byzantine Aqueduct of Valens to your right. Cross busy Atatürk Bulvarı and then head towards the aqueduct through this park. The huge monument in the middle of the park shows Mehment the Conqueror (Fatih) astride his horse.

6 Fatih İtfaiye

On the western edge of Fatih Anıt Park is this handsome Ottoman Revivalist building, which was designed by Greek architcet Konstantinos Kiriakidis and built in 1924 as the offices of the local *itfaiye* (fire brigade). Kiriakidis also designed the neighbouring building with its colourful tiled facade.

7 Kadınlar Pazarı

Continue through the aqueduct arch and into the Kadınlar Pazarı (p66) on İtfaiye Caddesi, a vibrant local local shopping precinct where there are a number of excellent eateries.

Best Walks
Bohemian Beyoğlu

🏃 The Walk

The streets running off İstiklal Caddesi are the traditional stamping ground of İstanbul's creative communities, and are littered with galleries, artists' ateliers, cafes, bars and boutiques as a consequence. This walk wends its way through the expat enclave of Cihangir, along the crooked laneways of Çukurcuma and into the music-filled streets of Tünel.

Start Taksim Meydanı; 🚋Taksim

Finish Galata Meydanı; 🚋Galata

Length 3km; three hours

🍴 Take a Break

Of the many stylish eating and drinking venues on Akarsu Yokuşu, our favourite is **Journey** (www.journeycihangir.com; Akarsu Yokuşu 21; breakfast ₺14-25, sandwiches ₺16-19, mains ₺16-39; ⏰9am-2am), a laid-back lounge cafe-bar serving Mediterranean comfort foods including sandwiches, soups, pizzas and pastas.

Galata Tower

❶ Taksim Meydanı

Set off from this busy square (p79), a popular meeting place for locals. The Atatürk Cultural Centre on its eastern edge is one of the city's most significant 20th-century buildings. It's currently closed for renovation.

❷ Cihangir Mosque

From Taksim Meydanı, walk south down traffic-choked Sıraselviler Caddesi and veer left into Arslan Yatağı Sokak. Follow it and Cihangir Caddesi to Susam Sokak, where you should turn right and then almost immediately left to admire a spectacular view of the Old City and Bosphorus from the garden terrace of this mosque.

❸ Kardeşler Cafe

Backtrack to Susam Sokak, turn left and follow Şimşirci Sokak, turning right into Akarsu Yokuşu and heading back towards Sıraselviler Caddesi. These streets are scattered with local cafes and bars, the most popular of which is this simple place next to the Firuz Ağa Mosque.

4 Faikpaşa Sokak

Walk past the mosque and turn right into Ağa Hamamı Sokak, passing the historic hamam that gives the street its name and then veering left into Faikpaşa Sokak, home to alluring antique shops including A La Turca (p96).

5 Museum of Innocence

Halfway down Faikpaşa Sokak, turn left and then right into Çukurcuma Caddesi. Continue downhill and you'll eventually come to a *çıkmazı* (cul de sac) where Orhan Pamuk's recently opened Museum of Innocence (p87) is located.

6 ARTER

Backtrack to Çukurcuma Caddesi, turn left and cross busy Yeni Çarşı Caddesi, continuing into Tomtom Kaptan Sokak and walking uphill past the rear of the Italian consulate until you reach İstiklal Caddesi. ARTER (p79), one of the city's leading contemporary art spaces, is to your left.

7 Galata Mevlevi Museum

Head left along İstiklal to Tünel Meydanı, named after its historic funicular. Turn into Galipdede Caddesi to find the Galata Mevlevi Museum (p86), set in a 15th-century *tekke* (dervish lodge).

8 Galata Tower

Continue down Galipdede Caddesi past the shops selling musical instruments to reach the avant-garde district of Galata, home to the landmark tower.

Best
Food

In İstanbul, meals are events to be celebrated. There's an eating option for every budget, predilection and occasion – all made memorable by the use of fresh seasonal ingredients and a local expertise in grilling meat and fish that has been honed over centuries. When you eat out here, you're sure to finish your meal replete and satisfied.

JULIAN LOVE/GETTY IMAGES ©

Traditional Eateries

Popular venues for lunch, which is often eaten out, include *lokantas* (eateries serving ready-made food), *pidecis* (Turkish pizza parlours), *kebapçıs* (kebap restaurants) and *köftecıs* (meatball restaurants). When not eating dinner at home, locals flock to *meyhanes* (taverns), where an array of hot and cold mezes (tapas-like dishes) are served. Fresh fish is enjoyed in *balık restorans* (fish restaurants) and meat in *ocakbaşıs* (fireside kebap restaurants).

Contemporary Cuisine

İstanbul has an ever-growing number of eateries serving modern Turkish cuisine. Many of these showcase food by chefs who draw inspiration from Turkey's diverse regional cuisines but do so with a European sensibility.

Street Food

Street vendors pound pavements across İstanbul, pushing carts laden with artfully arranged snacks. Look out for *simits* (sesame-encrusted bread rings), *mısır* (corn on the cob), *kestane* (chestnuts), *midye dolma* (stuffed mussels) and *çiğ köfte* (raw spiced meatballs). The most famous street snack of all is the *balık ekmek* (fish sandwich).

☑ Top Tips

▶ Popular restaurants are busy on Thursday, Friday and Saturday nights. Book ahead.

▶ Restaurant staff don't always speak English – ask staff at your hotel to make your booking.

▶ Alcohol is served in most restaurants reviewed in this book. Exceptions are noted.

Best Kebaps

Zübeyir Ocakbaşı
Succulent meats cooked over coals. (p88)

Gazientep Burç Ocakbaşı Tasty, expertly grilled meat in the heart of the Grand Bazaar. (p67)

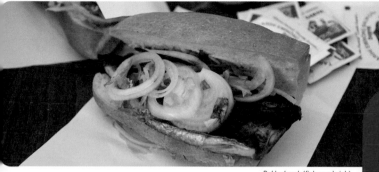

Balık ekmek (fish sandwich)

Şehzade Cağ Kebabı
Erzurum-style tender
lamb kebap. (p51)

Best Regional Food

Klemuri Delicious home-
style Laz dishes from the
Black Sea. (p88)

Antiochia Southeastern
dishes that look as good
as they taste. (p88)

**Siirt Şeref Büryan
Kebap** Tender slow-
cooked lamb from the
southeastern city of Siirt.
(p67)

**Best Modern
Turkish**

Lokanta Maya Stylish
bistro serving modern
takes on traditional
dishes. (p90)

Meze by Lemon Tree
Elegant surrounds, de-
lectable food and a good
wine list. (p89)

**Best Ottoman
Palace Cuisine**

Asitane Decadent dishes
once served to the sul-
tans. (p75)

Matbah Palace cuisine
in a garden setting.
(p51)

Best Cafe Food

Aheste House-made
cakes, quiches and light
dishes. (p90)

Enstitü Chic, well-priced
place with a seasonal
menu that changes daily.
(p90)

Best Baklava

Develi Baklava Tiny
place near the Spice
Market with a huge (and
well-deserved) reputa-
tion. (p63)

Karaköy Güllüoğlu The
perfect baklava stop at
any time of day. (p88)

Best Cheap Eats

Fatih Damak Pide
Everything a neighbour-
hood *pideci* should be,
and then some. (p66)

Dürümcü Raif Usta
Fast and fabulous kebap
wraps. (p67)

Aynen Dürüm Freshly
grilled meats and DIY
pickles. (p68)

Best
Drinking

İstanbul may be the biggest city in a predominantly Muslim country, but let us assure you that İstanbullus like nothing more than a drink or two. To join them, head to the bars and taverns found in Beyoğlu and along the Bosphorus. On the Historical Peninsula, the tipples of choice are çay (tea) or *Türk kahve* (Turkish coffee).

JUANMONINO/GETTY IMAGES ©

Rakı

Turkey's most beloved tipple is rakı, a grape spirit infused with aniseed. Similar to Greek ouzo, it's served in long thin glasses and drunk neat or with water, which turns the clear liquid chalky white.

Turkish Wine

Turkey grows and bottles its own *şarap* (wine), which is extremely quaffable but expensive due to high government taxes. If you want red wine, ask for *kırmızı şarap*; for white wine, *beyaz şarap*. As well as producing vintages of well-known grape varieties, Turkish winemakers also use local varietals including *boğazkere* and *buzbağ* (strong-bodied reds), *emir* (a light and floral white), *kalecik karası* (an elegant red) and *narince* (a fruity yet dry white).

Turkish Coffee

A thick and powerful brew, *Türk kahve* is drunk in a couple of short sips. If you order a cup, you will be asked how sweet you like it – *çok şekerli* means 'very sweet', *orta şekerli* 'middling', *az şekerli* 'slightly sweet' and *şekersiz* or *sade* 'not at all'.

Turkish Tea

Drinking çay is the national pastime. Sugar cubes are the only accompaniment and you'll find these are needed to counter the effects of long brewing, although you can always try asking for it *açık* (weaker).

☑ **Top Tips**

Though you shouldn't drink the grounds in the bottom of your cup of *Türk kahve*, you may want to read your fortune in them – check the Turkish Coffee/ Fortune Telling section of the website of İstanbul's longest-established purveyor of coffee, Kurukahveci Mehmet Efendi (www. mehmetefendi.com) for a guide.

NuTeras

Best Rooftop Bars

Mikla Spectacular views and a stylish clientele. (p91)

360 The city's most famous bar for good reason. (p91)

NuTeras Golden Horn views and a chic after-dinner club scene. (p93)

Cihannüma Amazing sunset views. (p37)

Best Street-Level Bars

Unter In the midst of the hipster enclave of Karaköy. (p92)

Cihangir 21 Laid-back neighbourhood bar in Cihangir. (p93)

Best Coffee

Manda Batmaz Traditional coffeehouse in Beyoğlu. (p90)

Fes Cafe Turkish coffee with a *lokum* (Turkish delight) chaser. (p68)

Karabatak Julius Meinl coffee and a bohemian vibe. (p92)

Best Tea

Dem Huge range of tea served in fine china cups. (p92)

Hazzo Pulo Çay Bahçesi One of Beyoğlu's few tea gardens. (p92)

Set Üstü Çay Bahçesi Fabulous views and pots of tea. (p52)

Best
Architecture

İstanbul is one of the world's great architectural time capsules. Here, locals still live within city walls built by Byzantine emperors, worship in Ottoman-era mosques and reside in grand 19th-century apartment buildings.

Byzantine Architecture

The city spent 1123 years as a Christian metropolis and many structures survive from this era. After the Conquest, numerous churches were converted into mosques; despite the minarets, you can usually tell a church-cum-mosque by its distinctive red bricks. The Byzantines also built aqueducts, cisterns and public squares that exist to this day.

Ottoman Architecture

After the Conquest, the sultans wasted no time putting their architectural stamp on the city, constructing mosques, palaces, hamams, *medreses* (theological schools) and *yalıs* (waterside timber mansions). The greatest of these buildings were commissioned by Süleyman the Magnificent and designed by his court architect, Mimar Sinan. Later sultans focussed their attentions on palaces and hunting lodges featuring ornate external detailing and ostentatious interior decoration; these and other buildings of the era have been collectively dubbed 'Turkish baroque'.

Ottoman Revivalism & Modernism

In the late 19th century, architects created a blend of European architecture alongside Turkish baroque, with some concessions to classic Ottoman style. This style has been dubbed 'Ottoman Revivalism' or First National Architecture. When the 20th century arrived and Atatürk proclaimed Ankara the capital of the republic, İstanbul lost much of its glamour and investment capital.

☑ Top Tips

▶ Architectural walking tours of the city are conducted by İstanbul Walks (www.istanbulwalks.com), a company run by a group of history, conservation and architecture buffs. Tours run daily and can be booked at short notice.

Best Byzantine Buildings

Aya Sofya One of the world's great buildings, with a magnificent interior. (p24)

Little Aya Sofya Exquisite church building now functioning as a mosque. (p35)

Basilica Cistern Extraordinary engineering and a

Beylerbeyi Palace

magnificent symmetrical design. (p30)

Rumeli Hisarı A massive structure strategically located on the narrowest point of the Bosphorus. (p110)

Best Ottoman Buildings

Topkapı Palace Pavilion-style architecture and a gorgeous landscaped setting. (p42)

Süleymaniye Mosque The greatest of the city's imperial mosques, with many intact outbuildings. (p60)

Blue Mosque A profusion of minarets, domes and fine İznik tilework. (p28)

Ayasofya Hürrem Sultan Hamamı Elegant

twin hamam built for a sultan's wife. (p126)

Kılıç Ali Paşa Hamamı A gorgeous hamam commissioned by an Ottoman admiral. (p126)

Best Turkish Baroque Buildings

Dolmabahçe Palace Imposing exterior and over-the-top interior decoration. (p100)

Beylerbeyi Palace Imperial splendour on the Asian shore of the Bosphorus. (p109)

Çırağan Palace Little sister to Dolmabahçe, possessing plenty of Ottoman opulence. (p106)

Küçüksu Kasrı Ornately designed imperial retreat built on the Bosphorus shore. (p110)

Best Contemporary Adaptive Reuse

SALT Galata 1892 bank building cleverly converted into gallery, library and restaurant spaces. (p83)

İstanbul Modern A shipping warehouse converted into a huge contemporary art gallery. (p80)

SALT Beyoğlu 1850s apartment block converted into a multilevel cultural centre. (p79)

Sakıp Sabancı Museum Sympathetic modern additions to one of the largest mansions on the Bosphorus. (p110)

Best
Hamams

IZZET KERIBAR/GETTY IMAGES ©

Succumbing to a soapy scrub in a traditional hamam (bathhouse) is one of the city's quintessential experiences. Not everyone feels comfortable with baring their bodies in public, though. In these cases, a private hamam treatment in one of the city's spas is a good alternative.

Bath Procedure

Upon entry you will be shown to a *camekan* (entrance hall), allocated a dressing cubicle and given a *peştemal* (bath wrap) and plastic sandals. Undress and put these on. Females may keep their knickers on, although this is optional. Males usually just wear the *peştemal* (but always leave it on). You'll then be shown to the *hararet* (steam room), where you can sit on the side or lie on top of the central *göbektaşı* (heated raised platform).

A traditional Turkish bath experience involves having an attendant wash, scrub and massage you. Soap, shampoo and towel are included in these treatments; you may wish to bring your own *kese* (exfoliating mitten).

Ayasofya Hürrem Sultan Hamamı (☎212-517 3535; www.ayasofyahamami.com; Aya Sofya Meydanı 2; bath treatments €85-170, massages €40-75; ☺8am-10pm; 🚇Sultanahmet) Meticulously restored twin hamam dating from 1556.

Kılıç Ali Paşa Hamamı (☎212-393 8010; http://kilicalipasahamami.com; Hamam Sokak 1, off Kemeraltı Caddesi, Tophane; self-service ₺100, bath service ₺130; ☺women 8am-4pm, men 4.30pm-midnight; 🚇Tophane) Recently restored and extremely beautiful 16th-century hamam.

Çemberlitaş Hamamı (☎212-522 7974; www.cemberlitashamami.com; Vezir Han Caddesi 8; self-service ₺60, bath, scrub & soap massage ₺90; ☺6am-midnight; 🚇Çemberlitaş) Gorgeous Ottoman twin hamam dating from 1584; best for a self-service bath.

Four Seasons Istanbul at the Bosphorus (☎212-381 4000; www.fourseasons.com/bosphorus; Çırağan Caddesi 28, Beşiktaş; 30/45min hamam experience €100/150; ☺9am-9pm; 🚇Bahçeşehir Unv or Çırağan) The perfect choice if you're looking for a luxury hamam experience.

Cağaloğlu Hamamı (☎212-522 2424; www.cagalogluhamami.com.tr; Yerebatan Caddesi 34; bath, scrub & massage packages €50-110; ☺8am-10pm; 🚇Sultanahmet) Twin 18th-century hamam with a magnificent interior; best for a self-service bath.

Best
Nargile Cafes

İstanbullus have perfected the art of *keyif* (quiet relaxation), and practise it at every possible opportunity. Nargile (water pipe) cafes are *keyif* central, offering their patrons pockets of tranquility off the noisy and crowded streets. Games of *tavla* (backgammon), glasses of tea, nargiles and quiet conversations are usually the only distractions on offer.

Ordering a Nargile

You'll need to specify what type of tobacco you would like. Most people opt for *elma* (when the tobacco has been soaked in apple juice, giving it a sweet flavour and scent), but it's possible to order it *tömbeki* (unadulterated) or in a variety of other fruit flavours. A nargile usually costs ₺20 to ₺25 and can be shared (you'll be given individual plastic mouthpieces).

Accompaniments

Locals usually drink çay when they are enjoying a nargile, beckoning the waiter over for regular refills. At the nargile cafes in Tophane, plates of fresh fruit and nuts are set up on each table – if you don't want to pay for this VIP option (usually around ₺50), specify that you only want a nargile and tea. Other snacks can be ordered with the waiter

Lale Bahçesi Located in a sunken courtyard in the shadow of the Süleymaniye Mosque. (p69)

Cafe Meşale Live music and a mixed crowd behind the Blue Mosque. (p37)

Best Beyoğlu Nargile Cafes

Tophane Nargile Cafes A cluster of *çay bahcesis* behind the Nusretiye Mosque in Tophane. (p93)

Best Old City Nargile Cafes

Erenler Nargile ve Çay Bahçesi Set in the vine-covered courtyard of the Çorlulu Ali Paşa Medrese near the Grand Bazaar. (p69)

Mimar Sinan Teras Cafe Panoramic water views and a predominantly student clientele. (p70)

Best
Museums & Galleries

İstanbul has always embraced art and culture. In Byzantine times, the emperors amassed huge collections of antiquities, importing precious items from every corner of their empire. The Ottoman sultans followed the same tradition, building extraordinary imperial collections. And these days the country's big banks and business dynasties vie to outdo each other in building and endowing galleries and cultural centres.

JULIAN LOVE/GETTY IMAGES ©

☑ Top Tips

▶ If you plan on visiting the major museums and monuments, the Museum Pass İstanbul (www. muze.gov.tr/museum_pass) will save you money and time.

Best Museums

İstanbul Archaeology Museums An extraordinary collection of antiquities, classical sculpture, historical artefacts and Ottoman tilework. (p46)

Museum of Turkish & Islamic Arts World-class collection of Oriental carpets. (p33)

Great Palace Mosaic Museum Showcases a stunning mosaic pavement dating from Byzantine times. (p33)

Museum of Innocence Orhan Pamuk's nostalgic museum/conceptual art project. (p87)

Carpet Museum A showcase of Anatolian carpets housed in three galleries in an 18th-century *imaret* (soup kitchen). (p49)

İstanbul Naval Museum Home to a spectacular collection of imperial caïques (ornately decorated wooden rowboats). (p105)

Best Art Galleries

İstanbul Modern Spotlights 20th-century Turkish painting alongside high-profile international artists. (p80)

ARTER Four floors of cutting-edge contemporary art on İstiklal Caddesi. (p79)

Pera Museum Turkey's most significant collection of Orientalist paintings. (p86)

SALT Beyoğlu Cultural centre with an emphasis on video and installation arts. (p79)

SALT Galata Visual arts exhibitions, lectures and performances. (p83)

Sakıp Sabancı Museum Hosts top-notch travelling international art exhibitions. (p110)

National Palaces Painting Museum Nineteenth-century Turkish paintings from the Dolmabahçe Palace collection. (p101)

Best
Views

Studded with historic minarets, domes and towers, the İstanbul skyline is the city's greatest asset. The hilly topography is fringed with waterways (the Bosphorus, Golden Horn and Sea of Marmara) and retains a surprisingly generous allocation of green spaces, including heavily treed parks and garden cemeteries. Together, these attributes offer views that are guaranteed to delight.

Scenic Viewpoints

The city's many hills are invariably crowned with Ottoman mosques, most of which incorporate scenic terraces. And these weren't the only Ottoman buildings that were designed to make the most of their location – imperial palaces and pleasure kiosks were almost always sited to take advantage of spectacular water vistas.

Rooftop Bars & Cafes

In İstanbul one of the most delightful experiences on offer is to enjoy a drink or meal in a rooftop cafe, bar or restaurant. Occupying the top floors of hotels and commercial buildings in Sultanahmet, Beyoğlu and along the Bosphorus shore, these venues give the city's eating and drinking scenes a unique allure.

Best Views from Monuments

Topkapı Palace Marble Terrace and Konyalı Restaurant Terrace. (p42)

Rumeli Hisarı Extraordinary Bosphorus views from the ramparts. (p110)

Dolmabahçe Palace The Bosphorus location ensures spectacular views. (p100)

Süleymaniye Mosque Golden Horn vistas from the terrace behind the mosque. (p60)

Best Restaurant, Cafe & Bar Views

Cihannüma One of the best views in the Old City. (p37)

Hamdi Restaurant Panoramic views of the Old City, Golden Horn and Bosphorus. (p66)

Mikla Spectacular 360-degree views across the city. (p91)

360 Across the Bosphorus to the Old City and Asian shore. (p91)

Duble Meze Bar Golden Horn views from the expansive terrace. (p89)

Mimar Sinan Teras Cafe Views of the Golden Horn and Bosphorus from the terrace. (p70)

Best
Shopping

Over centuries, İstanbullus have perfected the practice of shopping. Trading is in their blood and they've turned making a sale or purchase into an art form. Go into any carpet shop and you'll see what we mean – there's etiquette to be followed, tea to be drunk, conversation to be had. And, of course, there's money to be spent and made.

Bathwares

Towels, *peştemals* (bath wraps) and bathrobes made on hand looms in southern Turkey are popular purchases, as are olive-oil soaps and hamam sets (soap, exfoliation glove and hamam bowl).

Carpets & Kilims

The carpet industry is rife with commissions, fakes and dodgy merchandise, so you need to be extremely wary in all of your dealings.

Textiles

Turkey's southeast is known for its textiles, and there are examples aplenty on show in the Grand Bazaar. Also look for pashminas and shahtooshs (the real things, not cheap synthetic imitations) from the Subcontinent and decorative tribal textiles that have made their way here from Central Asia.

Ceramics

Many of the Turkish tiles and plates you see in the tourist shops have been painted using a silkscreen printing method and this is why they're cheap. Hand-painted pieces are more expensive.

Jewellery

Look for work by the city's growing number of artisans making contemporary pieces inspired by local culture.

JEN JUDGE/GETTY IMAGES ©

☑ **Top Tips**

▶ *Lokum* (Turkish delight) makes a great present for those at home. It's sold in speciality shops around the city.

Best Homewares

Hiç Designer homewares made by local and international artisans. (p83)

Özlem Tuna Superstylish homewares and jewellery sold from an atelier overlooking Sırkeci train station. (p53)

Tulu Cushions, bedding and accessories inspired by textiles from Central Asia. (p39)

Best Bathwares

Jennifer's Hamam Bath linens produced on

Ceramics for sale in a bazaar

old-style hand looms. (p38)

Abdulla Natural Products Stylish bath linens and pure olive-oil soap. (p70)

Derviş *Peştemals,* hamam bowls and feltwork. (p70)

Best Carpets & Kilims

Cocoon Textiles, rugs, scarves and handicrafts from Central Asia. (p38)

Mehmet Çetinkaya Gallery Heirloom rugs and textiles. (p39)

Dhoku Kilims featuring contemporary designs. (p72)

A La Turca Atmospheric Beyoğlu store full of antique kilims. (p96)

Best Jewellery

Ümit Berksoy Handmade Byzantine-style rings, earrings and necklaces. (p70)

Selda Okutan Sculptural pieces sold from the jeweller's atelier. (p97)

İKSV Tasarım Mağazası Pieces designed and made by local artisans. (p96)

Best Textiles

Muhlis Günbattı Fine cotton bedspreads and tablecloths embroidered with silk. (p72)

Yazmacı Necdet Danış Famous Grand Bazaar fabric store. (p72)

Mekhann Richly coloured hand-woven silk from Uzbekistan and a range of finely woven shawls. (p72)

Best Turkish Delight

Altan Şekerleme Cheap and deletable *lokum,* helva and *akide* (hard candy). (p72)

Lokum Boutique shop known for its exqulsile packaging. (p107)

Ali Muhiddin Hacı Bekir The most famous outlet, with branches in Eminönü and Beyoğlu. (p53)

Best Handicrafts

Ak Gümüş Central Asian tribal arts. (p73)

Beyoğlu Olgunlaşma Enstitüsü Beyoğlu retail outlet of local handicrafts school. (p95)

Nahıl Not-for-profit store selling handicrafts made by women from Turkey's economically disadvantaged east. (p95)

Best
Nightlife

There's a nightlife option for everyone in İstanbul. You can while away the night in a glamorous nightclub on the Bosphorus, listen to bands in a grungy Beyoğlu venue or drink rakı and burst into song at a cheap and rowdy *meyhane* (tavern) or *Türkü evi* (Turkish music bar).

Clubs

The best nightclubs are in Beyoğlu and on the 'Golden Mile' between Ortaköy and Kuruçeşme on the Bosphorus. Friday and Saturday are the busiest nights of the week and action rarely kicks off before 1am. Note that many of the Beyoğlu clubs close over summer, when clubbing action moves to coastal resorts south of the city or to the Golden Mile. Most of the Bosphorus clubs close over winter.

Live-Music Venues

Beyoğlu is the heart of the city's live-music scene, and clubs such as Babylon regularly program performances by live bands. But for a uniquely Turkish experience you should consider visiting a *Türkü evi*, where live *halk meziği* (folk music) is performed.

Meyhanes

On weekends locals like to get together with friends and family at *meyhanes*. Some *meyhanes* focus solely on food, but others host small groups of musicians who move from table to table playing *fasıl* music, emotion-charged Turkish folk or pop songs played on traditional instruments. These are favourites with large groups, who pay a set charge of ₺70 to ₺100 to enjoy a generous set menu with either limited or unlimited choices from the bar.

☑ **Top Tips**

▶ If you're keen to visit a Bosphorus club, consider booking to have dinner in its restaurant – otherwise you could be looking for a lucky break or a tip of at least ₺100 to get past the door staff.

▶ When İstanbullus go out clubbing they dress to kill. You'll need to do the same to get past the door staff at the Bosphorus clubs or into the rooftop bar-clubs in Beyoğlu.

Beyoğlu nightlife

Best Clubs

Babylon The best live-music venue in town. (p93)

MiniMüzikHol Hub of the avant-garde arts scene. (p92)

Indigo Dance-music enthusiasts congregate here on weekends. (p93)

Reina Queen of the Golden Mile superclubs. (p107)

Sortie Bosphorus views and celebrity clientele. (p107)

Kiki DJs and live sets; venues in Cihangir and Ortaköy. (p93)

Best Jazz Clubs

Nardis Jazz Club Long-running, intimate venue in Galata. (p94)

Nublu İstanbul İlhan Ersahin's ultra-cool basement venue in Karaköy. (p94)

Worth a Trip

Going into its second decade, **Love Dance Point** (☎212-232 5683; www.lovedp.net; Cumhuriyet Caddesi 349, Harbiye; ⊙11.30pm-5am Fri & Sat; Ⓜ Taksim or Osmanbey) is easily the most Europhile of the local gay venues, hosting musical icons and international circuit parties. Hard-cutting techno is thrown in with gay anthems and Turkish pop, attracting a varied clientele. You'll find it in the suburb of Harbiye, a short walk from Taksim Meydanı.

Best
For Kids

If you're after a family-friendly city break, İstanbul is the perfect choice. Your children might whinge about the number of mosques and museums on the daily itinerary, but they'll be quickly appeased by the fantastic baklava, *lokum* (Turkish delight) and *dondurma* (ice cream) to be sampled, not to mention the castles, underground cisterns and parks to be explored.

Best for Toddlers

Gülhane Park Playground equipment and plenty of open space. (p49)

Hippodrome Loads of open space to run around in. (p33)

Ferry Trips Little ones love climbing aboard the city's fleet of ferries. (p141)

Best for Bigger Kids

Bosphorus Cruise Spot monuments from both sides of the boat. (p108)

Rumeli Hisarı Kids love castles! Just be careful that junior knights and princesses don't go too close to the edge on the battlements. (p110)

Basilica Cistern It's creepy (way cool), and kids can explore the walkways suspended over the water. (p30)

Hafız Mustafa Cakes, pastries and ice cream. Yum. (p52)

Best for Teenagers

İstanbul Modern Plenty of exhibits – including lots of multimedia – that will amuse and engage. (p80)

☑ **Top Tips**

▶ Children under 12 years receive free or discounted entry to most museums and monuments.

▶ Kids under seven travel free on public transport.

▶ Most pavements are cobbled, so strollers aren't very useful – bring a backpack carrier instead.

Best
For Free

The hippies and backpackers who flocked to İstanbul in the 1960s and 1970s would certainly blow their meagre budgets if they headed this way today. Fortunately, the ever-increasing price of hotel rooms, transport and meals is counterbalanced by an array of top-drawer sights that can be visited at no cost. These include galleries, museums, churches, mosques and tombs.

Best Byzantine Sights

Little Aya Sofya Built by order of the Emperor Justinian and now functioning as a mosque. (p35)

Best Tombs

Aya Sofya Tombs Ottoman tiles, calligraphy and decorative paintwork. (p33)

Tomb of Sultan Ahmet I Decorated with fine 17th-century İznik tiles. (p29)

Tombs of Süleyman & Roxelana Superb 16th-century tiles and stained glass. (p61)

Best Galleries & Museums

ARTER One of the most prestigious art venues in town, with an international exhibition program. (p79)

SALT Exciting cultural centres in Beyoğlu (p79) and Galata (p83).

Carpet Museum Allowed free admission at the time of research, although a fee may be levied in future. (p49)

Pera Museum Free admission every Friday between 6pm and 10pm; Wednesdays also free for students. (p86)

Best Bazaars & Markets

Grand Bazaar One of the world's oldest and most atmospheric shopping malls. (p56)

Spice Bazaar Join the crowds at this ancient marketplace near the Eminönü docks. (p66)

Balık Pazarı Beyoğlu's historic produce market sells much more than *balık* (fish). (p79)

Karaköy Balık Pazarı The catch of the day is sold on the shore of the Golden Horn (p83).

Kadınlar Pazarı Fresh produce market in Fatih where local *kadınlar* (women) do their daily shopping. (p66)

Best
Culinary Walks & Cooking Classes

İstanbul Eats (http:// istanbuleats.com) The seriously committed foodies at this highly recommended company offer a number of culinary walks through city neighbourhoods including the Old City, Bazaar District and Beyoğlu. Also on offer is a tour to the Karaköy Balık Pazarı and Kadıköy Fresh Produce Market; a day spent exploring Beşiktaş, Üsküdar and Kuzguncuk; and a market experience and cooking class in Kurtuluş, near the Golden Horn.

Turkish Flavours
(☎ 0532 218 0653; www. turkishflavours.com; tour per person US$145) This well-regarded outfit offers food tours visiting the Spice Bazaar, a farmers' market and the Kadıköy Fresh Produce Market; a street-food walk in Kadıköy; and a home-cooked dinner in an 1880 Beyoğlu house. Cooking classes concentrating on traditional home-cooked Turkish dishes are also offered.

Cooking Alaturka
(☎ 0536 338 0896; www. cookingalaturka.com; Akbıyık Caddesi 72a, Cankurtaran; cooking class per person €65; 🚊 Sultanahmet) Dutch-born Eveline Zoutendijk opened the first English-language Turkish cooking school in İstanbul in 2003 and since then has built a solid reputation for her convivial classes, which offer a great introduction to Turkish cuisine and are suitable for both novices and experienced cooks. The delicious results are enjoyed over a five-course meal in the school's restaurant.

Istanbul Walks (☎ 212-516 6300; www.istanbul-walks.com; 2nd fl, Şifa Hamamı Sokak 1; walking tours €30-80, child under 6yr free; 🚊 Sultanahmet) Best known for its expertly guided walking tours focussing on history and architecture, İstanbul Walks also offers a 'Dining Out in a Turkish Way' tour that visits a *simit* (bread ring) bakery,

CHRIS CHEADLE/GETTY IMAGES ©

a traditional coffeehouse, an *ocakbaşı* (kebap restaurant where the meat is cooked over coals), a *meyhane* (tavern) and an *işkembecisi* (eatery selling tripe soup).

Survival Guide

Survival Guide

Before You Go

When to Go

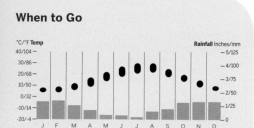

°C/°F Temp
Rainfall Inches/mm

→ Spring (Mar–May)
Possibly the best time of the year to visit; tulips bloom in April.

→ Summer (Jun–Aug)
The heat can seem unrelenting, but shoulder-season hotel rates and the İstanbul Music Festival compensate.

→ Autumn (Sep–Nov)
A lovely time of year, with gentle breezes and a profusion of cultural festivals.

→ Winter (Dec–Feb)
Winters are often bone-chillingly cold. Low-season rates apply in hotels except over the Christmas/New Year period.

Book Your Stay

→ Staying in Sultanahmet makes sense if you plan to spend most of your time visiting museums and the bazaars. Beyoğlu is a better option for those interested in eating, drinking and clubbing.

→ Book your room as far in advance as possible, particularly if you are visiting during the high season (Easter–May, September–October and Christmas/New Year).

→ Many hotels offer a discount of between 5% and 10% for cash payments. Room rates in the low season (November–Easter, excluding Christmas/New Year) and shoulder season (June–August) are often discounted.

→ A Value-Added Tax (VAT) of 8% is added to all hotel bills; it's usually included in the price quoted when you book.

→ Many hotels provide a free airport transfer from

Atatürk International Airport if you stay three nights or more.

→ Breakfast is almost always included in the room rate.

→ Rental apartments are rarely in blocks with elevators – be prepared for steep stairs if you've booked something with a view.

→ For author recommendation reviews and online booking check Lonely Planet's website: www.lonelyplanet.com.

Best Budget

Cheers Hostel (www.cheershostel.com) Airy dorm rooms, streetside terrace and a lovely winter lounge.

Hotel Alp Guesthouse (www.alpguesthouse.com) Budget prices but midrange facilities, including a wonderful roof terrace.

Hotel Peninsula (www.hotelpeninsula.com) Simple, but comfortable, rooms and a friendly atmosphere.

Marmara Guesthouse (www.marmaraguesthouse.com) Friendly, family-run choice.

Best Midrange

Hotel Empress Zoe (www.emzoe.com) Keenly priced rooms and slightly more expensive suites overlooking a courtyard garden.

Hotel İbrahim Paşa (www.ibrahimpasha.com) Exemplary boutique hotel with wonderful roof terrace.

Hotel Uyan (www.uyan-hotel.com) The lower end of the midrange, with some super-cheap singles.

Marmara Pera (www.themarmarahotels.com) Five-star location and facilities for three-star prices.

Sarı Konak Hotel (www.istanbulhotelsarikonak.com) Elegant choice with good amenities.

Sirkeci Mansion (www.sirkecimansion.com) Fantastic service, facilities and entertainment program.

Best Top End

Four Seasons Istanbul at the Bosphorus (www.fourseasons.com/bosphorus) The city's best

hotel, with a wonderful pool terrace.

Tom Tom Suites (www.tomtomsuites.com) Elegant suite rooms and a rooftop restaurant with spectacular views.

Sumahan on the Water (www.sumahan.com) Understated luxury on the Bosphorus, complete with a private motor launch.

Witt Istanbul Hotel (www.wittistanbul.com) Huge, super-stylish suites and a great breakfast.

Best Apartment Rentals

istanbul!place Apartments (http://istanbulplace.com/) Stylish and well-set-up apartments in the Galata district.

Manzara Istanbul (www.manzara-istanbul.com) Locations in Galata, Cihangir and Kabataş.

1001 Nites (www.1001nites.com) Locations in Sultanahmet, Çukurcuma and Cihangir.

Galateia Residence (www.galateiaresidence.com) Well-located long-term luxury apartments perfect for business-people.

Arriving in İstanbul

☑ **Top Tip** For the best way to get to your accommodation, see p17.

Atatürk International Airport

➡ **Atatürk International Airport** (IST, Atatürk Havalimanı; ☏212-463 3000; www.ataturkairport.com) is 23km west of Sultanahmet; the *dış hatlar* (international terminal) and *iç hatlar* (domestic terminal) are side by side.

➡ A taxi costs around ₺45 from the airport to Sultanahmet, ₺55 to Taksim Meydanı (Taksim Sq).

➡ An efficient metro service (₺4) travels between the airport and Zeytinburnu, from where it's easy to connect with the tram (₺4) to Sultanahmet, Eminönü and Kabataş. From Kabataş, there's a funicular (₺4) to Taksim Meydanı. The metro station is on the lower ground floor beneath the international departures hall – follow the 'Metro/Subway' signs down the escalators and through the underground walkway. Services depart every two to 10 minutes or so from 6am to midnight. The entire trip takes approximately 60 minutes to Sultanahmet, 70 minutes to Eminönü and 95 minutes to Taksim.

➡ If you're staying in Beyoğlu, take the Havataş Airport Bus (₺10). This travels between the arrivals hall and Cumhuriyet Caddesi, next to Taksim Meydanı, every 30 minutes between 4am and 1am; the trip takes between 40 minutes and one hour, depending on traffic.

Sabiha Gökçen International Airport

➡ **Sabiha Gökçen International Airport** (SAW, Sabiha Gökçen Havalimanı; ☏216-588 8888; www.sgairport.com) is 50km east of Sultanahmet, on the Asian side of the city, and is popular with cut-price European carriers.

➡ A taxi costs around ₺130 from the airport to Sultanahmet, ₺100 to Taksim Meydanı.

➡ The Havataş Airport Bus (₺13) travels from the airport to Taksim Meydanı in Beyoğlu between 4am and 1am. The trip takes approximately 90 minutes. If you're heading towards Sultanahmet, you'll then need to take the funicular (₺4) to Kabataş and the tram (₺4) from Kabataş. There's also a service to Kadıköy (₺8, 4.15am to 12.45am).

Getting Around

Tram

☑ **Best for...** Travelling between Sultanahmet and Beyoğlu.

➡ An excellent *tramvay* (tramway) service runs from Bağcılar, in the city's west, to Zeytinburnu (where it connects with the metro from the airport) and onto Sultanahmet and Eminönü. It then crosses the Galata Bridge to Karaköy (to connect with the Tünel) and Kabataş (to connect with the funicular to Taksim Meydanı). A second service runs from Cevizlibağ, closer to Sultanahmet on the same line, through to Kabataş.

→ Services run every five minutes from 6am to midnight.

→ The fare is ₺4; *jetons* (transport tokens) are available from machines on every tram stop.

Funicular

☑ **Best for...** The steep uphill climb from all tram stops to İstiklal Caddesi.

→ A funicular saves passengers the steep walk from Karaköy to İstiklal Caddesi. Known as the Tünel, the three-minute service (₺4) operates every five or 10 minutes from 7am to 10.45pm.

→ Another funicular connects the Kabataş tram stop with the metro station at Taksim Meydanı. The service operates between 6am to midnight and *jetons* cost ₺4.

Ferry

☑ **Best for...** Sightseeing and travelling on the Bosphorus and Golden Horn (Haliç).

→ The main ferry docks are at the mouth of the Golden Horn (Eminönü and Karaköy) and at Beşiktaş, a few kilometres northeast of Galata

Bridge, near Dolmabahçe Palace. There are also busy docks at Kadıköy and Üsküdar on the Asian (Anatolian) side. Ferries travel many routes around the city, but the following routes are those commonly used by travellers:

→ **Eminönü–Anadolu** Kavağı (Long Bosphorus Tour); one or two services per day.

→ **Eminönü–Kadıköy** Approximately every 15 to 20 minutes from 7.30am to 9.10pm.

→ **Eminönü–Üsküdar** Approximately every 20 minutes from 6.35am to 11pm.

→ **Karaköy–Kadıköy** Approximately every 20

minutes from 6.20am to 11pm.

→ **Üsküdar–Karaköy– Eminönü–Kasımpaşa– Hasköy–Ayvansaray– Sütlüce–Eyüp** The Golden Horn (Haliç) ferry; hourly from 7.30am to 7.45pm, fewer services on Sunday.

→ *Jetons* cost ₺4 for most trips and it's possible to use İstanbulkarts on all routes except the Bosphorus tours. The main ferry company is **İstanbul Şehir Hatları** (İstanbul City Routes; www.sehirhatlari. com.tr), but Turyol and Dentur Avraysa also offer Bosphorus cruises and services between the European and Asian shores.

Tickets & Passes

Rechargeable İstanbulkart travel cards can be used on most trams, ferries, buses and metro services, and offer a considerable discount on fares. They can also be used to pay for fares for more than one traveller (one swipe per person per ride).

The cards can be purchased from machines at metro and funicular stations for a nonrefundable charge of ₺10, which includes ₺4 in credit. If you buy yours from a street kiosk near a tram or bus stop, you will pay ₺8 (no credit).

Cards can be recharged with amounts between ₺5 and ₺150 at kiosks or at machines at ferry docks, metro and bus stations.

Taxi

☑ **Best for...** Travelling at night or if you are short on time.

➡ Taxi rates are very reasonable (from Sultanahmet to Taksim Meydanı will cost around ₺15) and there are no evening surcharges.

➡ Ignore taxi drivers who insist on a fixed rate as these are much higher than you'd pay using the meter; steer clear of the taxi drivers waiting for fares next to Aya Sofya Meydanı, as they are often rip-off merchants.

➡ Note that few of the city's taxis have seatbelts.

➡ If you take a taxi over either of the Bosphorus bridges it's your responsibility to cover the toll (₺3.40). The driver will add this to the fare.

Metro

☑ **Best for...** Trips to the airport.

➡ Metro services leave every two to 10 minutes between 6am and midnight. *Jetons* cost ₺4. Go to www.istanbul-ulasim.com.tr for maps of the metro network.

➡ The M1A connects Aksaray with the airport, stopping at 15 stations including the *otogar* (main bus station) along the way. There are plans to add a link between Aksaray and Yenikapı, southwest of Sultanahmet.

➡ The M2 connects Yenikapı with Taksim, stopping at three stations along the way: Vezneciler, near the Grand Bazaar; on the new bridge across the Golden Horn (Haliç); and at Şişhane, near Tünel Meydanı in Beyoğlu. From Taksim, another service travels northeast to Hacıosman via nine stations.

➡ A fourth line known as the Marmaray connects Kazlıçeşme, west of the Old City, with Ayrılak Çeşmesi, on the Asian side. This travels via a tunnel under the Sea of Marmara, stopping at Yenikapı, Sirkeci and Üsküdar en route and connecting with the M4 metro running between Kadıköy and Kartal.

Bus

☑ **Best for...** Exploring the Bosphorus villages.

➡ The major *otobus* (bus) stations are at Taksim Meydanı (underground), Beşiktaş, Eminönü, Kadıköy and Üsküdar.

➡ Most services run between 6am and 11pm.

➡ You must have an İstanbulkart before boarding.

➡ For bus timetables and route details, see the website of the **İstanbul Elektrik Tramvay ve Tünel** (İETT, Istanbul Electricity, Tramway and Tunnel General Management; www.iett.gov.tr).

Essential Information

Business Hours

☑ **Top Tip** Final entry to most museums is generally an hour before the official closing time. We have cited the former time in our reviews.

Opening hours vary wildly across businesses and services in İstanbul. The following is a very general guide:

Post offices & banks 8.30am to 5pm Monday to Friday

Shops 9am to 6pm Monday to Saturday

Restaurants & cafes Breakfast 7.30am to

10.30am, lunch noon to 2.30pm, dinner 6.30pm to 10pm

Bars Afternoon to early morning

Nightclubs 11pm to late

Electricity

230V/50Hz

Emergency

Ambulance (📞112)

Fire (📞110)

Police (📞155)

Tourist Police (📞212-527 4503; Yerebatan Caddesi 6)

Money

➡ The currency is the Türk Lirası (Turkish Lira; ₺).

➡ ATMS are widely available.

➡ Most hotels, car-rental agencies, shops, pharmacies, entertainment venues and restaurants accept Visa and MasterCard; Amex isn't as widely accepted and Diners is often not accepted. Inexpensive eateries usually accept cash only.

➡ The 24-hour *döviz büro-sus* (exchange bureaux) in the arrivals halls of the international airports usually offer competitive rates.

➡ Tip 10% in restaurants and ₺2 per bag for bell-boys; in taxis round up the fare to the nearest ₺1.

Public Holidays

New Year's Day 1 January

National Sovereignty & Children's Day 23 April

Labor & Solidarity Day 1 May

Commemoration of Atatürk, Youth & Sports Day 19 May

Victory Day 30 August

Republic Day 29 October

Religious festivals are celebrated according to the Muslim lunar Hejira calendar; two of these festivals (Şeker Bayramı and Kurban Bayramı) are also public holidays. Şeker Bayramı is a three-day festival at the end of Ramazan (Ramadan), and Kurban Bayramı, the most important religious holiday of the year, is a four-day festival whose dates change each year. During these festivals, banks and offices are closed and hotels, buses, trains and planes are heavily booked.

Money-Saving Tips

➡ If you plan to visit three or more museums, purchase a Museum Pass İstanbul (p144).

➡ The İstanbulkart offers a considerable discount on public-transport fares (₺2.15 as opposed to the usual ₺4, with additional transfers within a two-hour journey window; ₺1.60 for the first transfer, ₺1.50 for the second and ₺1.30 for the third).

➡ Check if your hotel offers free airport pick-ups and drop-offs.

Safe Travel

Theft is not generally a big problem and robbery (mugging) is comparatively rare, but take normal precautions. Areas to be particularly careful in include Aksaray/Laleli (the city's red-light district), the historic city walls, the Grand Bazaar (pickpocket central) and the streets off İstiklal Caddesi in Beyoğlu.

Be careful when crossing roads – cars often won't slow for pedestrians.

Telephone

Mobile Phones

➡ To use a local SIM in a phone you've bought from home, you'll need to register the phone. This is a complicated and time-consuming procedure if you're only here for a short time, so it's easiest to use international roaming on your home phone or purchase a mobile phone and local SIM in İstanbul. To do the latter, ask the staff to organise the activation of the SIM for you (you'll need to show your passport); the account should activate within a few hours.

➡ Turkey uses the standard GSM network operating on 900Mhz or 1800Mhz, so not all US and Canadian phones work here. Check with your provider before leaving home.

Phone Codes

If you are in European İstanbul and wish to call a number in Asian İstanbul, you must dial 📞0, followed by 📞216. If you are in Asian İstanbul and wish to call a number in European İstanbul, dial 📞0 followed by 📞212. Do not use a prefix (that is, don't use the 📞0 or 📞212/6) if you are calling a number on the same shore. Local mobile numbers start with a four-digit code beginning with 📞05.

Country code 📞90

Intercity code 📞0 + local code

International access code 📞00

Toilets

Most hotels, restaurants and museums offer Western-style toilets; public toilets and those in mosques are often of the squat variety.

Tourist Information

The Ministry of Culture & Tourism operates four tourist information offices or booths in the city; a fifth is scheduled to open at some stage in the future inside the Atatürk Cultural Centre

Museum Pass İstanbul

Valid for 72 hours from your first museum entrance, the **Museum Pass İstanbul** (www. muze.gov.tr/museum_pass) costs ₺85 and allows entrance to Topkapı Palace and Harem, Aya Sofya, the İstanbul Archaeology Museums, the Museum of Turkish and Islamic Arts, the Great Palace Mosaics Museum and the İstanbul Museum of the History of Science & Technology in Islam. Purchased individually, admission fees to these sights will cost ₺125, so the pass represents a saving of ₺40. It can be purchased from some hotels and also from the ticket offices at Topkapı Palace, Aya Sofya, the Great Palace Mosaics Museum and the İstanbul Archaeology Museums.

on Taksim Meydanı in Beyoğlu. All can provide a free map of the city.

Sultanahmet (Map p32; ☎212-518 8754; Hippodrome, Sultanahmet; ☉9.30am-6pm mid-Apr–Sep, 9am-5.30pm Oct–mid-Apr; 🚇Sultanahmet)

Sirkeci train station (Map p48; ☎212-511 5888; Sirkeci Gar, Ankara Caddesi, Sirkeci; ☉9am-6pm mid-Apr–Sep, 9am-5.30pm Oct–mid-Apr; 🚇Sirkeci)

Karaköy (Karaköy International Maritime Passenger Terminal, Kemankeş Caddesi, Karaköy; ☉9.30am-5pm Mon-Sat; 🚇Karaköy)

Atatürk International Airport (☎212-465 3547; International Arrivals Hall; ☉9am-9pm)

Travellers with Disabilities

➡ İstanbul can be challenging for mobility-impaired travellers. Roads are potholed and pavements are often crooked and cracked. Fortunately, the city is making attempts to rectify this.

➡ Government-run museums are free of charge for disabled visitors. Topkapı Palace, the İstanbul Archaeology Museums,

Mosque Etiquette

➡ Remove your shoes before walking on the mosque's carpet; you can leave them on shelves near the mosque door or place them in one of the plastic bags provided and carry them with you.

➡ Women should always cover their heads and shoulders with a shawl or scarf; both women and men should dress modestly.

➡ Avoid visiting mosques at prayer times – within 30 minutes of when the ezan (call to prayer) sounds from the mosque minaret – and also around Friday lunch, when weekly sermons and group prayers are held.

➡ Speak quietly and don't use flashes on your camera if people are praying.

İstanbul Modern and the Pera Museum have wheelchair access and accessible toilets. The last three of these sights also have limited facilities to assist accessibility for vision-impaired visitors.

➡ All public transport is free for the disabled; the metro and tram can be accessed by people in wheelchairs.

➡ **FHS Tourism and Event** (www.accessibleturkey.org) is an İstanbul-based tour agency that has a dedicated department organising accessible travel packages and tours.

Visas

➡ At the time of research, nationals of the following countries (among others) could enter Turkey for up to three months with only a valid passport (no visa required): Denmark, Finland, France, Germany, Greece, Israel, Italy, Japan, New Zealand, Russia, Sweden and Switzerland.

➡ Nationals of the following countries (among others) needed to obtain an electronic visa (www.evisa.gov.tr) before their visit: Australia, Canada, China, Ireland, Mexico, Netherlands, Spain, UK and USA. These visas arre valid for between 30 and 180 days and for either a single entry or a multiple entry, depending on the nationality. Visa fees cost US$15 to US$60 depending on nationality.

➡ Chinese and Indian nationals need to 'meet certain conditions' before being granted an electronic visa.

➡ Your passport must have at least six months'

validity remaining, or you may not be admitted into Turkey. See the website of the **Ministry of Foreign Affairs** (www.mfa.gov.tr) for the latest information.

Language

Pronouncing Turkish is pretty simple for English speakers as most Turkish sounds are also found in English. If you read our pronunciation guides as if they were English, you should be understood just fine. Note that the symbol **ew** represents the sound 'ee' pronounced with rounded lips (as in 'few'), and that the symbol **uh** is pronounced like the 'a' in 'ago'. The Turkish **r** is always rolled and **v** is pronounced a little softer than in English. Word stress is quite light in Turkish in our pronunciation guides the stressed syllables are in italics.

To enhance your trip with a phrasebook, visit **lonelyplanet.com**. Lonely Planet iPhone phrasebooks are available through the Apple App store.

Basics

Hello.
Merhaba.   mer·ha·ba

Goodbye. (when leaving)
Hoşçakal.   hosh·cha·kal

Goodbye. (when staying)
Güle güle.   gew·le gew·le

Yes.
Evet.   e·vet

No.
Hayır.   ha·yuhr

Please.
Lütfen.   lewt·fen

Thank you.
Teşekkür   te·shek·kewr
ederim.   e·de·reem

Excuse me.
Bakar mısınız.   ba·kar muh·suh·nuhz

Sorry.
Özür dilerim.   er·zewr dee·le·reem

How are you?
Nasılsınız?   na·suhl·suh·nuhz

Fine, and you?
İyiyim, ya siz?   ee·yee·yeem ya seez

Do you speak English?
İngilizce   een·gee·leez·je
konuşuyor   ko·noo·shoo·yor
musunuz?   moo·soo·nooz

I don't understand.
Anlamıyorum.   an·la·muh·yo·room

Eating & Drinking

The menu, please.
Menüyü   me·new·yew
istiyorum.   ees·tee·yo·room

What would you recommend?
Ne tavsiye   ne tav·see·ye
edersiniz?   e·der·see·neez

I don't eat (meat).
(Et) yemiyorum.   (et) ye·mee·yo·room

I'd like (a/the) ...
... istiyorum.   ... ees·tee·yo·room

a (cup of) coffee
bir (fincan) kahve   beer (feen·jan) kah·ve

a (jug of) beer
bir (fıçı) bira   beer (fuh·chuh) bee·ra

Enjoy your meal.
Afiyet olsun.   a·fee·yet ol·soon

Cheers!
Şerefe!   she·re·fe

That was delicious!
Nefisti!   ne·fees·tee

The bill, please.
Hesap lütfen.   he·sap lewt·fen

Shopping

I'd like to buy ...
... almak | al·*mak*
istiyorum. | ees·tee·yo·room

I'm just looking.
Sadece | sa·de·*je*
bakıyorum. | ba·*kuh*·yo·room

How much is it?
Ne kadar? | ne ka·*dar*

It's too expensive.
Bu çok pahalı. | boo chok pa·ha·*luh*

Do you have something cheaper?
Daha ucuz | da·ha oo·*jooz*
birşey var mı? | beer·*shay* var muh

Emergencies

Help!
İmdat! | eem·dat

Call a doctor!
Doktor çağırın! | dok·tor cha·*uh*·ruhn

Call the police!
Polis çağırın! | po·*lees* cha·*uh*·ruhn

I'm lost.
Kayboldum. | kai·bol·*doom*

I'm ill.
Hastayım. | has·*ta*·yuhm

Where's the toilet?
Tuvalet nerede? | too·va·*let* ne·re·de

Time & Numbers

What time is it?
Saat kaç? | sa·*at* kach

It's (10) o'clock.
Saat (on). | sa·*at* (on)

in the morning
öğleden evvel | er·le·*den* ev·vel

in the afternoon
öğleden sonra | er·le·*den* son·ra

in the evening
akşam | ak·*sham*

now
şimdi | sheem·dee

yesterday	*dün*	dewn
today	*bugün*	boo·*gewn*
tomorrow	*yarın*	ya·*ruhn*
1	*bir*	beer
2	*iki*	ee·*kee*
3	*üç*	ewch
4	*dört*	dert
5	*beş*	besh
6	*altı*	al·*tuh*
7	*yedi*	ye·*dee*
8	*sekiz*	se·*keez*
9	*dokuz*	do·*kooz*
10	*on*	on

Transport & Directions

Where is the (market)?
(Pazar yeri) | (pa·*zar* ye·*ree*)
nerede? | ne·re·de

What's the address?
Adresi nedir? | ad·re·*see* ne·deer

Can you show me (on the map)?
Bana (haritada) | ba·*na* (ha·ree·ta·da)
gösterebilir | gers·te·re·bee·leer
misin? | mee·seen

Please put the meter on.
Lütfen | lewt·fen
taksimetreyi | tak·*see*·met·re·yee
çalıştırın. | cha·luhsh·*tuh*·ruhn

I'd like a ticket to ...
... bir bilet | ... beer bee·*let*
lütfen. | lewt·fen

Does it stop at ...?
... durur mu? | ... doo·*roor* moo

I'd like to get off at ...
... inmek | ... een·*mek*
istiyorum. | ees·tee·yo·room

Behind the Scenes

Send Us Your Feedback

We love to hear from travellers – your comments help make our books better. We read every word, and we guarantee that your feedback goes straight to the authors. Visit **lonelyplanet.com/contact** to submit your updates and suggestions.

Note: We may edit, reproduce and incorporate your comments in Lonely Planet products such as guidebooks, websites and digital products, so let us know if you don't want your comments reproduced or your name acknowledged. For a copy of our privacy policy visit lonelyplanet.com/privacy.

Our Readers

Many thanks to the travellers who used the last edition and wrote to us with helpful hints, useful advice and interesting anecdotes:

Andrew Mangion Randon, Bente Jensen, Kirti Tawde, Liz Temple, Vivek Shinde

Virginia's Thanks

Many thanks to Pat Yale, Mehmet Umur, Emel Güntaş, Faruk Boyacı, Atilla Tuna, Tahir Karabaş, Jen Hartin, Eveline Zou-tendijk, George Grundy, Barbara Nadel, Ercan Tanrıvermiş, Ann Nevans, Tina Nevans, Jennifer Gaudet, Özlem Tuna, Ansel Mullins, Ken Dakan and the many others who shared their knowledge and love of the city with me.

Acknowledgments

Cover photograph: Blue Mosque, Naomi Parker

This Book

This 5th edition of Lonely Planet's *Pocket İstanbul* guidebook was researched and written by Virginia Maxwell. The previous two editions were also written by Virginia. This guidebook was commissioned in Lonely Planet's London office, and produced by the following:

Destination Editor Jo Cooke **Coordinating Editor** Kristin Odijk **Product Editor** Elin Berglund **Senior Cartographer** Corey Hutchison **Book Designer** Virginia Moreno **Assisting Editors** Justin Flynn, Kate Mathews **Cover Researcher** Naomi Parker **Thanks to** Bruce Evans, Ryan Evans, Larissa Frost, Jouve India, Claire Naylor, Karyn Noble

Index

See also separate subindexes for:

🟦 **Eating p152**

🔴 **Drinking p152**

✳️ **Entertainment p153**

🔶 **Shopping p153**

Our Writer

Virginia Maxwell

Although based in Australia, Virginia spends much of her year researching guidebooks in the Mediterranean region. Of these, Turkey is unquestionably her favourite. As well as working on the previous two editions of this guide, she also writes Lonely Planet's İstanbul city guide, covers İstanbul, Thrace and Marmara for the *Turkey* guide, and writes about the city for a host of international magazines and websites. Virginia usually travels with partner Peter and son Max, who have grown to love Turkey as much as she does.

Published by Lonely Planet Publications Pty Ltd
ABN 36 005 607 983
5th edition – Feb 2015
ISBN 978 1 74321 561 6
© Lonely Planet 2015   Photographs © as indicated 2015
10 9 8 7 6 5 4 3 2 1
Printed in China